通天之書 The Divine Book

by Sheng-yen Lu

A US Daden Culture Publication

US Daden Culture LLC
3440 Foothill Blvd.
Oakland, CA 94601
U.S.A.
Website: www.usdaden.com
Email: us.daden.culture@gmail.com

© 2014 by Sheng-yen Lu

The right of Living Buddha Lian-sheng, Sheng-yen Lu to be identified as author of this work including all translations based on his original writings, has been asserted by him in accordance with the Copyright, Designs, and Patents Act 1988.

All rights reserved. No part of this book may be reproduced in any form or by any means, electronic or mechanical, including photography, recording, or by any information storage or retrieval system or technologies now known or later developed, without permission in writing from the publisher.

Lu, Sheng-yen, 1945-
The Divine Book/by Sheng-yen Lu;
translated by DJ Chang, Gillian Yu, Yongbin Liu, Meiling Kang, and Shizhong Duan;
edited by DJ Chang, Wilhall Lee, Shelley Higgins, Jessie Loh, Belinda Liu, Marc Streich, and Yongbin Lin;
proofread by Shelly Higgins, Phoebe Tan, Janet Ho, Roger Ost, and Raymond To.

Library of Congress Control Number (PCN): 2014936792
ISBN-13: 978-0-9960699-0-8
ISBN-10: 0996069909
1. True Buddha School. 2. Chinese-Tantrayana Buddhism.
Cover design and layout by US Daden Culture Design Team
Photograph by US Daden Culture
Set in Minion Pro 12
US Daden books are printed on acid-free paper and meet the guidelines for the permanence and durability set by the Council of Library Resources.

Printed in the U.S.A.

Special Acknowledgements

The True Buddha Translation Teams (TBTTs) would like to express the highest honor and deepest gratitude to Living Buddha Lian-sheng Sheng-yen Lu and Master Lianxiang for their continuing support and guidance on the translation effort. Without their compassion, wisdom, blessings, and encouragement, this project would not have reached fruition.

In addition, we would like to acknowledge the diligent work put forth by the following volunteers on this project: the leader of US Daden, Master Lianseng; DJ Chang, Gillian Yu, Yongbin Liu, Meiling Kang, and Shizhong Duan (translators); DJ Chang, Wilhall Lee, Shelley Higgins, Jessie Loh, Belinda Liu, Marc Streich, and Yongbin Lin (editors); Shelly Higgins, Phoebe Tan, Janet Ho, Roger Ost, and Raymond To (proofreaders); Yee Lin Lee (quality control); and Renee Cordsen (publication). We would like to thank these dedicated and selfless volunteers who have contributed their time and effort to promote the works of Living Buddha Lian-sheng, and to support the publications of US Daden Culture.

We would also like to extend our sincere appreciation to all other volunteers who work behind the scenes, facilitating the translation process, and handling administrative responsibilities.

May all volunteers be blessed with immeasurable merits. May all sentient beings benefit from the ocean of wisdom.

Table of Contents

Preface: The Divine Book   1
1. Nine Dragons   5
2. Flying Over Buddha Mountain   9
3. A Pig Demon   13
4. The Divine Book   17
5. Ten Feet Tall   21
6. Worm Cave   25
7. The Washer Woman   29
8. White Tara   33
9. Jade Pond Pure Land   37
10. Seeing Fengfeng   41
11. Zen Discussion With Fengfeng   45
12. Buddha King of the Era   49
13. Willy-Nilly Heaven   53
14. Princess Wencheng   57
15. Encountering Bi Gan   61
16. The Stranger Xu You   65
17. Fond of the Willy-Nilly Heaven   69

18. Senlou Palace	73
19. Five Direction Deities of Plague	81
21. Divination of Future Fortune or Not	85
22. The Patriarch Bodhidharma Said as Such	89
23. What do Sutras Explain?	93
24. Bodhiruci	97
25. The Buddha, Bodhidharma, and Grand Master Lu	101
26. A Cure for Chronic Ringworm	105
27. Cancer "Breaker"	109
28. True "Brainwashing"	113
29. Hurry Off, Dragon King	117
30. The Snake and Mouse	121
31. A Thunder Rumbling Day	125
32. A Sudden "Impulse"	129
33. Tanzhe Temple	133
34. The Deity of Nine Planets	137
35. Never Descend to Four Births	141
36. Red-eyes	145
37. The Queen of Indra	149
38. The Vajra Throne	153
39. Enlightened as Buddha's Enlightenment	157
40. Three Little Black Dogs	161

41. Discussion about Desire with Fengfeng 165
42. Copper Body Iron Bone Talisman 169
43. Typhoon Fengshen 173
44. Search for Zheng Cheng Gong 177
45. California's Huge Earthquake 181
46. I Heard a Woman Cry 185
Glossary 189

Preface: The Divine Book

One day, while in deep meditation, I experienced an unusual and unprecedented incident.

At first, surrounded by complete darkness without any trace of light, I felt that I was dropping fast, as if on a roller coaster. Besides being dizzy, my body felt like a piece of falling leaf. A sinister wind seemed to be blowing from all directions.

When I stopped falling and landed, I looked around and saw a small speck of light shining in the west. The closer I moved towards the west the larger the light grew. I walked forward along the tortuous path.

Suddenly, I arrived at a prison built from solid steel and iron bars.

Inside the locked jail were two fierce-looking and nude "Raksasis."

The Raksasis said to me, "Grand Master Lu, please let us out. We have been locked inside here by Shakyamuni Buddha for over two thousand years. If you don't help us this time we will never be let go. We are so fortunate that Grand Master Lu appeared today. We would appreciate your letting us out as soon as possible."

I felt compassion for them.

Hence opened the prison gate. Unexpectedly, the moment the gate opened, the two flew out in a northwesterly direction following a chilly wind.

At that same moment, a celestial child appeared. His face was like a full moon and he wore his hair in two buns. He yelled loudly to me, "This is bad! This is bad! Something very wrong happened! Something very wrong happened!"

I questioned, "What went wrong?"

The celestial child answered, "These two Rakshasis were "Sundarī" and "Zhànzhē." They were interfering with Shakyamuni Buddha's attempt at saving sentient beings. The two female demons made Shakyamuni Buddha notorious. But today, you Grand Master Lu released them. This is a significant mistake."

I replied, "Since I freed them, surely they will correct themselves and cease misbehaving."

The celestial child responded, "You are wrong, Grand Master Lu. The two female devils will not ever consider changing. Devils are devils. They won't change. You should have never, never released them."

I answered, "Let it be since I have already let them go."

The celestial child said, "Grand Master Lu, you freed the two Rakshasis. Later you will learn how they can stand in the way of your saving sentient beings."

The release of the two Rakshasis was no longer on my mind. If they truly "return my favor with meanness," then it will be my fate. I won't complain if this is my fate.

I fully understand that an enlightened one can be seriously challenged by devils. If there is no interference from the devil, how can one become a Buddha?

Poem:

When do the ups and downs end in a life span?
The only way is through self-purification.
The more sentient beings you save,
The more entwined you will end up,
Between truth and lies.
Your mind and heart must be unaffected.
(This book contains many extraordinary stories. It will be great loss if you do not read them!)

Not only will you make yourself reach enlightenment, but you will also enlighten your students.

Sheng-yen Lu

1. Nine Dragons

Once again, during meditation, I was led by an angelic child to a majestic hall. After entering the hall and looking around, I soon realized that it was a kitchen. What fascinated me was that, although there were many cups and plates in there, each cup was filled with celestial nectar and divine juice; and each plate was filled with every kind of heavenly food and exotic fruit.

Placed among the plates was a steamer with the lid on. Steam was spewing out of the steamer meaning that the food was cooked.

I could not help feeling hungry when seeing it. My stomach was growling and saliva almost drooled from my mouth.

The celestial child asked,

"Grand Master Lu, what do you like to eat most?'

I replied, "Red turtle pastry." (In Taiwanese)

The fairy child said,

"This steamer contains food made from red turtle pastry. It tastes perfect since it is just the right chewiness for you."

The fairy child lifted the cover, and behold I saw ten small dragons made from the same kind of material that "red turtle pastry" is made

from. Nine of the ten were cyan and one was black.
The ten dragons looked like lizards, tongues, or pens.
The celestial child explained,
"Grand Master Lu, don't feel strange. Human beings draw dragons based on their own imagination. What you see now is what dragons really look like."

Since I was very hungry, I ignored using any manners, and ate the nine cyan dragons one after another. As I was reaching for the tenth black dragon,

The fairy child said, "Hold on, you don't want to eat the black dragon."

I asked, "Why not?"

The child responded, "Your having eaten the nine cyan dragons symbolizes that you will write like flying dragons. You will save sentient beings with your penmanship. You are going to write continuously, spread the word of the true Buddhadharma, and inspirational writing will emerge from you like water flowing from a spring. It will never dry up, like having the power of nine soaring dragons."

He added, "However, the black dragon is prepared to be eaten by those who will defile you. Once they eat the black dragon, their heart will turn black. Likewise they will blacken your name, and stop you from saving sentient beings."

After hearing what he said, I was stunned.

I asked, "What should I do??"

The child answered, "Your fate has already been determined. Nothing you do now will alter it. This is how life is. Since you have nine cyan dragons surely you can win over the one black dragon, can't you? It would be too big a joke in the human world if you were to lose to one black dragon when you have nine cyan ones behind you."

Indeed I was embarrassed after hearing what he said.

The celestial child gave me some respite when he said, "Life is never perfect in the saha red dust of the human realm. If perfection does ex-

ist, then it would be blissful paradise. Grand Master Lu with these nine cyan dragon pens your literary accomplishments will be outstanding."
"Will the black devil dragon be my calamity?" I asked.
"Yes, it will."
"Can it be avoided?"
"No!" the fairy child replied, "You, Grand Master Lu, must be enlightened. Once you are enlightened, the black dragon cannot affect you at all. Not only will you make yourself reach enlightenment, but you will also enlighten your students."

Poem:

Buddha tolerated insults in the past.
While Lian Shen practices defamation-bearing today.
Even though being spit on by everyone,
Not a single word will he return to them.

Listen carefully; non-attached on either side means having a view of the Middle Way.

Sheng-yen Lu

2. Flying Over Buddha Mountain

Once again, the angelic child beckoned me. This time he led me to a lofty mountain, a truly huge mountain soaring high into the sky.

I glanced around and noticed the awe-inspiring scenery. The mountain was formed of numerous layers of oddly shaped rock. Pine and cypress trees provided bursts of emerald green shade. The mountain sides were also graced with springs of crystal clear water. Majestic carpets of perennial flowers were all blossoming together. Flying birds were chirping. The sound of water falling echoed like cries of fierce dragons. Up and down both sides of the mountain were endless rows of exquisite trees.

I asked the celestial child, "What mountain is this?"

The divine child answered, "This is Buddha Mountain!"

On hearing that the name of the mountain was Buddha Mountain I immediately put my palms together and prepared to kneel down in offering the three formal head-touching bows.

The celestial child stopped me and said, "Wait, although Buddha is the name of the mountain it is only a name. On the surface, it sounds elegant and looks neat and attractive. But in reality, it contains mountain demons and water devils. There are also cow-like beasts, snake fiends, tree devil spirits, and rock demons hidden in it.

I was so astonished by what the child was saying that I could only stammer and not say a word.

The celestial child added, "Today, the saha world has no truly real Buddhism. They are all packaged and only present an outer appearance. They only provide lip service and operate by theory alone. None of them are actually enlightened and practice cultivation with sincerity.

By now I was perspiring profusely!

The angelic child continued, "Today, I see only one rare cultivator who practices daily in earnest and is a genuine no-mind practitioner."

"Who is it?" I enquired.

"It is you Grand Master Lu!"

I replied, "I don't ever mind."

I truly do not mind.

The celestial child responded, "It is because you have no mind, that you are a no-mind practitioner."

The child continued, "Let us cross over the mountain."

Right away, a small auspicious cloud appeared under the heavenly child's feet. Supporting the child it emitted a million colorful beams while floating in space.

The heavenly youngster said to me, "Why are you not up here yet? Indeed you are a Padmakumara!"

In the blink of an eye, a large white lotus manifested under my feet and lifted me up flying. One behind the other, we glided up and over Buddha Mountain.

With curiosity I questioned the angelic child, "Is it true that there is no one of no-mind on Buddha Mountain?"

The divine child replied, "Listen carefully; non-attached on either side means having a view of the Middle Way. When one's consciousness reaches the treasure of consciousness, it is called consciousness-only. In the world, there are few who do not mind about any of this; you are one of the few."

"Yet sentient beings despise me"

The divine child answered, "That is why it is absolute."

I retorted, "Neither did I keep the absolute in my mind."

The angelic child responded, "Absolute but not absolute makes absolute."

Poem:

Buddha Mountain appears splendid,
Who knows that it is rather withered?
Sentient beings notice only superficiality,
Wind blows the scent of a plum blossom.

The saha world is originally an unreal world.
You will find many impostors of you.

Sheng-yen Lu

3. A Pig Demon

In the past, there was a joke. A person put down another by saying, "You are a pig!"

The victim of this slander responded, "I am not a pig!"

And from then on he inherited the nickname "Not a Pig." Indeed the nickname "Not a Pig" became so popular that everyone began calling him "Not a Pig" instead of his real name.

The situation became so unbearable for him that he finally gathered all the local neighbors and friends and held a meeting with the intention of restoring his real name.

But when he got to the podium the first sentence out of his mouth was, "I am really, truly, and absolutely *not*, not a pig!"

As soon as he finished the sentence, the audience below him burst into even greater laughter.

And in the end, he was still "Not a pig".

***

Enough of these nonsensical tales. During meditation, an angelic child and I flew over Buddha Mountain and continued onward.

Another person appeared and moved toward us.

Not only was this person riding on a lotus flower as I was but he also closely resembled me. We stared at each other.

I said to him, "I am Lu Sheng-yen. Who are you?"

He replied, "I am Lu Sheng-yen. Who are you?'

"I am Padmakumara!"

"I am Padmakumara!"

This was devastating to me! Here was an impostor who had taken my name and miserably looked like me.

I performed the Padmakumara mudra. But he did too.

He muttered to himself and then threw a "golden brick" which transformed into a golden beam of light that came crashing down in an instant to batter my head.

It happened too quickly for me to dodge. I thought my head would be crushed and bleeding from the blow and that I would certainly die from the attack! But just in time, the celestial child opened a cloth bag. From it radiated blue-green lights which intercepted the golden brick and pulled the brick into the bag.

Moreover, the fairy child calmly took a mirror out of his sleeve. The mirror flashed one time.

The flash transformed him back into his true persona, a pig. After the mirror flashed on him three times he caught fire and turned into roast pork. He howled horribly and eventually disintegrated into dust.

I questioned the divine child, "Who was that?"

The child answered, "A pig demon."

"Why did he pretend to be Padmakumara and Lu Sheng-yen?"

The godlike youngster replied,

"The saha world is originally an unreal world. You will find many impostors of you. They can claim to be Padmakumara, your dharma brother, your sister, your duplicate, your relative, or your master. However, it is quite easy to tell the fakes from the real one."

"How so?" I asked.

The celestial child answered, "You will know he is authentic if he is not greedy, has no temper, and is not ignorant. On the contrary, if he acts greedy, angry, and ignorant, then he must be an imposter."

I asked, "What about your cloth bag?"

The immortal kid replied, "It belongs to Maitreya Buddha."

I questioned, "And the mirror?"

The divine child answered, "It is a demon-exposing mirror."

Poem:

> *A cultivator walks the right path.*
> *Needs nothing therefore will not be disgusted.*
> *Breaks off greed, anger, ignorance, and affection.*
> *The pig demon dies in front of the mirror.*

When worldly associations are fully understood, in the eyes of the righteous, it is all but a joke.

Sheng-yen Lu

4. The Divine Book

The angelic child and I arrived at a site in the heavenly realm. There were exotic flowers and exquisite grasses everywhere. Belvederes and pavilions were built using the seven precious jewels. The air was imbued with the brilliance of rainbow hues, saturated with abundant auspicious energy, and effused with a rich fragrance that was both extremely pleasant and soothing.

I asked the young immortal, "Where are we?"

The angelic child answered, "At the Site of Grand Dignity."

We walked over to a large pavilion. On it, was a sign that read, "Vairocana Pavilion of Grand Dignity."

However, the doors appeared to be tightly shut. I turned my head to look at the young celestial child, but he had already vanished from the spot.

I thought for a moment. The name Vairocana Pavilion of Grand Dignity sounded quite familiar. Then all at once I recalled that this was the fiftieth place where the Sudhana studied.

Indeed this was the Pavilion of Maitreya.

The angelic child had to be the Maitreya in disguise. No wonder he carried Maitreya's cloth sack.

It then dawned on me.

I snapped my fingers three times at the pavillion doors. They opened. I entered and looked around. It was truly amazing. Inside was an entirely different region! The size of the pavilion was immeasurable and indescribable. It was more awe-inspiring than any fairyland.

I saw many large Bodhisattvas. Some of them I knew. Others I did not. There were large numbers of them.

I arrived at the Bright Seven Golden Mountain, and met the wondrously radiant Dignified and Powerful Godly King Maitreya Buddha.

Maitreya Buddha said, "Do you know why I disguised myself as an angelic child and led Grand Master Lu here?"

I answered, "No, I do not."

Maitreya Buddha continued, "It is only because I felt sorry for you and your many adverse encounters in the saha world. Therefore, I led you here so that you can bathe in the Buddha's radiance and rest a moment."

I then asked, "What is my future like?"

Maitreya Buddha answered, "Like a sea with high waves."

"What about a sea with high waves?"

Maitreya Buddha replied, "You can be master of all states."

I replied, "Maitreya Buddha, thank you for your guidance." (Being master of all states means being liberated.)

Maitreya Buddha said, "I have *The Divine Book* and would like to present it as a gift to you. Put it in your heart. Whenever you are in trouble, open and read the book, and you will then be able to resolve the problem. *The Divine Book* can make all your wishes come true and reverse adversity into auspicious events. It contains thousands upon thousands of methods which in turn solve thousands upon thousands of misfortunes. It will help you save sentient beings."

Just then Maitreya Bodhisattva emitted a white beam and *The Di-*

vine Book instantly entered my heart. My heart then began to radiate continuously.

As soon as I received *The Divine Book* there was nothing I did not know, and nothing I did not understand.

My understanding is: When worldly associations are not yet fully comprehended, everything is either "right or wrong" or "one or another." Yet none of them are true.

When worldly associations are fully understood, in the eyes of the righteous, it is all but a joke.

I "act without demanding anything in return."

Poem:

> *"The Divine Book" is a precious jade book.*
> *Its splendor and wonder are without measure.*
> *One is enlightened once it opens.*
> *Know the long and the short of it.*

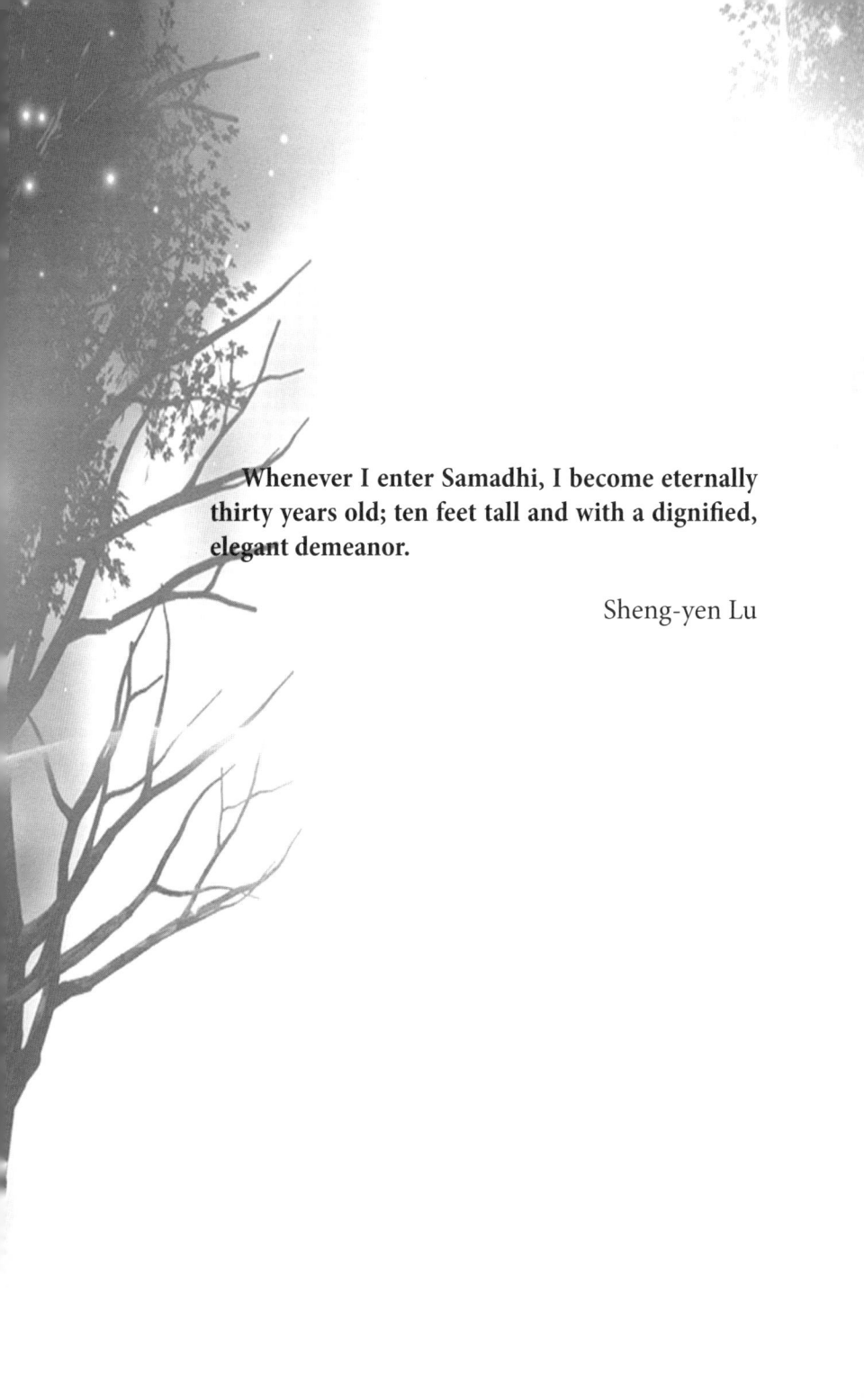

Whenever I enter Samadhi, I become eternally thirty years old; ten feet tall and with a dignified, elegant demeanor.

Sheng-yen Lu

5. Ten Feet Tall

In my current incarnation in the human realm, because I lacked adequate nutrition as a youngster, by the age of thirty I had only reached a height of one hundred and sixty-two centimeters. This was short. And by the time I reached forty I had become slightly chubby.

However, when my illusory body appears after entering Samadhi, it is no longer one hundred and sixty-two centimeters or chubby.

Instead, it is ten feet tall! My face is radiant and appears almost as if I wear make up. My nose is straight now and my mouth is perfectly shaped. My teeth are white and my ears distinctive. My eyes are clear with elegant eyebrows, and I am adorned in a white velvet robe.

My illusory body is about thirty years old. Not only does it exhibit the wisdom of someone well-educated but it also has the charm and charisma of a young hero. Whenever I enter Samadhi, I become eternally thirty years old; ten feet tall and with a dignified, elegant demeanor.

Having said that, the second time I entered a very deep meditation, my ten-foot-tall illusory body appeared. I saw a white rabbit not far away in front of me. This rabbit was not a common rabbit. It shone with an awesome brilliance. I wondered, wasn't this the famous Jade

Rabbit of the Moon Palace?

The Jade Rabbit acted strangely. It appeared to want to lead me somewhere. Its head kept turning back towards me. When I stopped walking, the Jade Rabbit stopped. As soon as I began to move to follow it, the Jade Rabbit would start to hop forward.

When the Jade Rabbit jumped up to the sky, I too followed and jumped high.

As soon as we reached a palace, the rabbit naturally disappeared.

I did not hurry in at first. I stayed outside admiring the exquisitely ornate wall carvings and artwork.

I then saw a colorful painting. On it was a lady sitting on a Taihu stone. Her face was so beautiful and faultless that no other like it could be found in the human realm.

The splendid depiction of her clothes could not hide her slender stature. Her curves were perfectly convex and concave. Her figure was shapely.

The colors were whiter than white and redder than red making the whole painting come alive.

Indeed it drew my attention so much that I felt my soul leave my body.

Just then I saw the lady in the painting looking at me with her sparkling eyes, calmly calling out to me, "Grand Master Lu!"

I responded, "Who are you?"

"Reiyui."

Lady Reiyui moved her body making one side of the Taihu stone available, indicating that she wanted me to sit down next to her.

I sat down without thinking twice. Lady Reiyui then leaned against me. I immediately smelled her fragrance and could see her rose and snow white colored face with small cherry-like mouth coming closer to me. Her nostrils and mouth were slightly open.

With a tantalizing voice Lady Reiyui said, "Grand Master Lu, you are mine!"

Moving seductively, her face red and panting she let her fine white skin brush against my body.

I almost lost myself!

At that very moment the Jade Rabbit appeared right in front of me, made eye contact with me and rolled his eyes back and forth to get my attention. This calmed me down and brought me back to reality.

Once more I looked at Lady Reiyui beside me, I was startled. She had changed into an old haggard woman with white hair, wrinkled skin, and swollen body. She smelled foul and was drooling dirty yellow saliva...

Quickly I pushed her away. She then began to shrivel up, decay, and fall.

The colorful drawings on the palace walls disappeared and the palace vanished. The Jade Rabbit winked in front of me as if laughing at my lack of meditative fortitude.

I did not know what had just happened.

Poem:

> *Enticed by a siren.*
> *One cannot allow one's mind to run loose.*
> *Meditation is of utmost importance.*
> *Lose your footing and your heart trembles.*

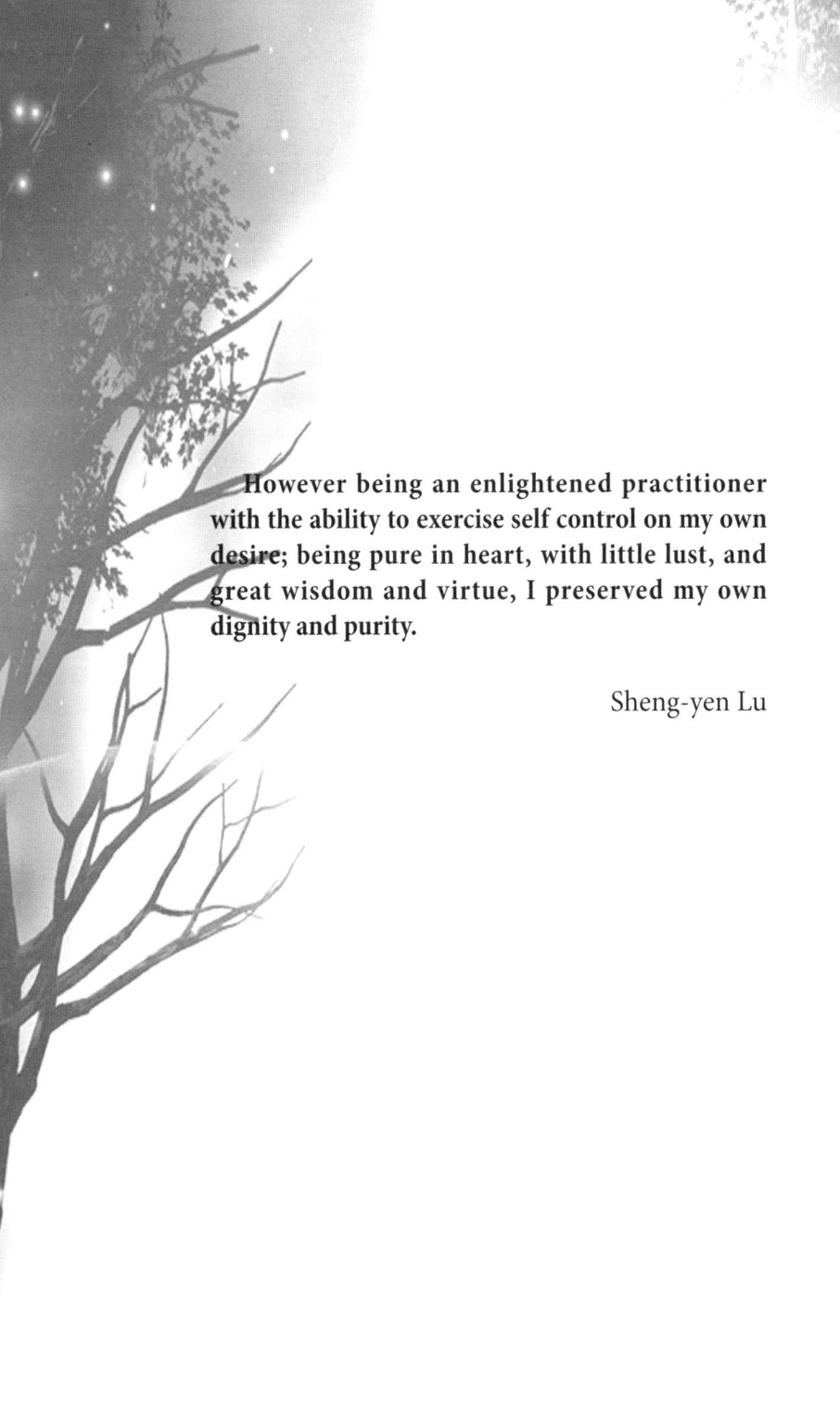

However being an enlightened practitioner with the ability to exercise self control on my own desire; being pure in heart, with little lust, and great wisdom and virtue, I preserved my own dignity and purity.

Sheng-yen Lu

6. Worm Cave

I must say, that the Jade Hare was quite agile! He directed me to yet another palace. This time, written on the palace, were the two characters: "Lust Palace."

At second glance, I saw that there was a tablet to the one side on which several lines were written, and they were shocking. The lines read:

In this world, humans are obliged to live with life's daily difficulties and challenges. Everything is a worry. There is no trace of joy.

Only one thing can bring joy to one's life, "lust," and the act of copulation between a man and a woman. That solves one's anxieties.

One is born out of desire! One also dies by desire!

People should understand that lust is non-poisonous; so what is it about lust that we fear?

People should also be aware that lust can be poisonous, so we must not get addicted.

If males are not overdoing it and females are not under-doing it, then there will be no spinsters at home and no bachelors beyond the eligible age outside the home. Then, the world is in check!

After reading these lines, I pondered how true they were. They appeared valid but were actually fallacious. The problem is that worries can only be solved temporarily, not forever.

Though I have to acknowledge that to worldly people, a man and woman making love is the a most joyful act.

I then entered the Lust Palace with the Jade Hare. What I saw and heard turned my face and ears red and caused my heart to race.

It was because the entire Lust Palace looked as if:

Intoxicating fumes flowed upward. Vast quantities of golden guns were everywhere. Each gun attack was followed by moans and cries. People were divided into five colors and held down in five directions. They adopted every kind of strange and unusual posture. Two objects turned and rolled. Each pair's eyes seemed drunk and stupefied.

I watched in awe!

I also saw the postures:

Vertical Butterfly Seeking Nectar, Lost Bird Finding a Nest, Bee Producing Honey, Double Dragons Fighting the Pearl, Racing Hungry Horse, and ....

These postures were done standing, sitting, lying, or up-side down.

None did not titillate one's eyes!

Listening to the various sounds intensified the effect. My legs became weak:

Moaning and sighing sounds;
Mosquitoes and buzzing sounds;
Hungry and ravenous sounds;
Sudden and tidal wave sounds;
Singing and humming sounds;
Dead and alive sounds.

There were excited souls begging to die; dreaming of fantasies to come; beaming with joy; calm after the exhausting moves.

Seeing all these, my own desires also emerged subconsciously and it became very difficult for me to resist them. A stunningly beautiful naked woman came close to me.

At that very moment, I remembered that I am a practitioner. I recalled *The Divine Book* bestowed by Maitreya.

Consulting *The Divine Book*, it revealed one character, "restore."

I shouted, "Restore!"

I turned to look again at the creatures in the Lust Palace.

What was the Lust Palace had turned into a worm cave. Those turning, rolling bodies were now all white worms!

Two white worms were copulating.

Thousands and thousands of white worms were all engaged in coitus.

I thought, if I had acted the same, I would have been just like a worm.

However being an enlightened practitioner with the ability to exercise self control on my own desire; being pure in heart, with little lust, and great wisdom and virtue, I preserved my own dignity and purity.

Poem:

> *Sink into the sand dust and transform into a worm.*
> *When does persistent desire rest?*
> *Saints and sages can alter karma and practise self-restraint.*
> *Break forever the bitterness and sorrow in life.*

I knew that this world is simply a stage for the various forms of past and future.

Sheng-yen Lu

7. The Washer Woman

The Jade Hare and I arrived at a new location. A wide river ran alongside it. Its flowing water gave off a murmuring sound. The sun's rays reflected off its surface and shining with hints of red. By the river was a forest that was mostly hidden. Growing near the forest were abundant flowers that seemed unusually bright and cheery. It was an enchanting view!

We walked to a small dirt road by the river; by it was a brook that emerged from a fork in the river. Near the brook, we came across a young washer woman. She was squatting down while washing a cloth.

Serene surroundings made quite a picture. I greeted the washer woman.

She raised her head and looked at me. She was smiling; her eyes were crystal clear and beautiful.

She had shiny black hair that reached her fair neck. Her face appeared to be sweet, yet intelligent. Her red lips were voluptuous and attractive. Her eyebrows long and fine; her hands soft and slender, and her skin clean and smooth. The washer woman was agile.

Although she was wearing an ordinary long skirt while washing, it did not hide her exquisitely curvaceous figure.

As she squatted, her calf showed and it was white as snow.

Nothing would have happened if I had simply passed through and not stopped.

But the washer woman stood up suddenly. I caught a glimpse of the gleam from her moist cherry lips.

Her black eyes sparkled.

Her fine neck was elegant.

Her clothing was dishevelled revealing her deep cleavage.

She asked me, "Where do you come from? Where are you going?"

I answered, "I am a practitioner. I come from nowhere and am going nowhere."

She then asked, "I heard that practitioners are not allowed to look directly at women; that practitioners cannot touch a female body. Is this true?"

(She was very bold.)

I responded, "In theory, yes."

She said, "Why then do you stare at me?"

I did not know how to respond.

She said, "I want to touch your hand!"

She was not at all shy. Gracefully, with both her hands, she held my hands with my palms tightly together. She said, "Come closer!"

Her left thigh pressed lightly against my right foot.

I smelled an unknown fragrance. Not knowing when, I grabbed her hands. Her body came even closer. My blood started to seethe.

She motioned to me that there was a private wood close by. I noticed her half-closed eyes filling with the hunger and thirst of desire.

Then suddenly, I saw a fish inside *The Divine Book*. A dead smelly fish with tarnished eyes taking its last breath.

(*The Divine Book* indicated to me that this fish was either her previous reincarnation or it would be her next life.)

My desire declined. If ..., I would have been the same, a fish!

Then all at once, what I was holding in my hands was a dry piece of

a withered leaf. What was on my right foot was a withered leaf!
I knew that this world is simply a stage for the various forms of past and future. Am I also a fish?

Poem:

> *Momentary joy and excitement;*
> *Shackling future lives with relentless affinity.*
> *An enticing washer woman's appearance cannot be pursued;*
> *Karma would have been added if not for "The Divine Book."*

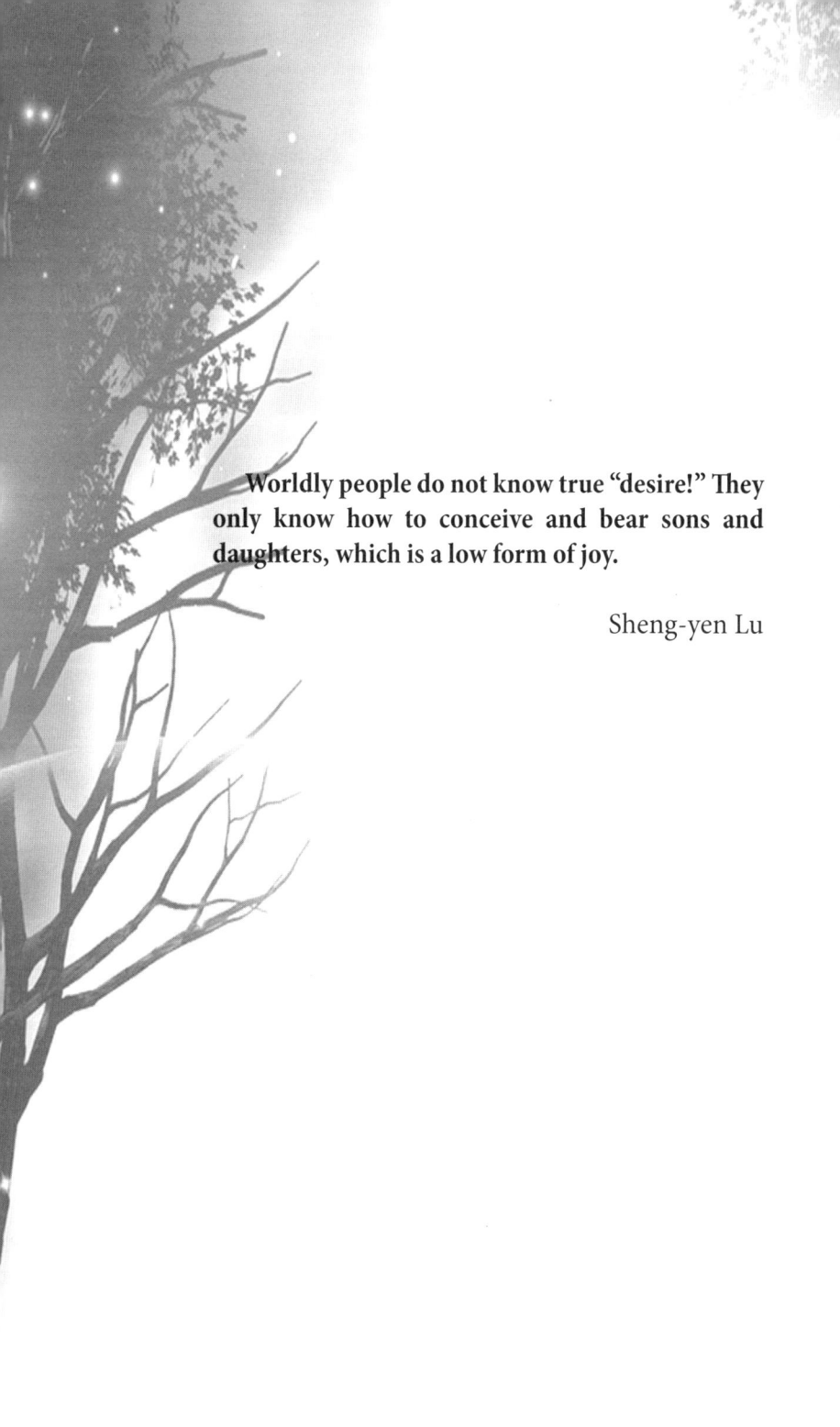

Worldly people do not know true "desire!" They only know how to conceive and bear sons and daughters, which is a low form of joy.

Sheng-yen Lu

8. White Tara

The Jade Hare led me to the Ao Ming Celestial Palace. In the palace, I met the White Tara.

The Tantric White Tara has an image of: a body white as snow, one head with two arms; the right hand in the wish-granting mudra, and the left in the flower-holding mudra holding three blue poppies, one a bud, one in half bloom, and one in full bloom.

She has one eye in each palm, the soles of the feet, and the brow chakra for a total of seven eyes.

She is a young lady wearing a celestial cloth and silk skirt adorned with various jade-pearl gems.

However, the White Tara that I saw was: oval faced, with tapered shoulders, a thin waist, slender, and radiant; with apricot eyes, lips like ruby, thin long eyebrows, and snow white skin; pretty breasts, a willowy posture, a passionately delicate body and elegant nature; a smooth and striking nose, cheeks as red as fresh lychees, with the fetching freshness of Spring, and also remarkably charming and cute.

The White Tara and I had a relationship from a previous existence.

As soon as the White Tara scattered the blue poppies, they formed into circles and layer by layer, and on their own, built a Flower Palace.

At once the flowers became radiant, shining brightly all at the same time.

The White Tara and I united together and became one - yoga.

This is precisely how it felt:

Fluttering of celestial sleeves; the fragrance of rich hyacinths; seemingly moving lotus flower; overflowing with flower dew; dimpled smiles like a fresh spring peach; the swirling wind and dancing snow; running through fields of flowers; angry as well as happy; united with one another, as if flying and soaring; smooth lips and moist tongue; sparkling speech; fully bloomed spring plum blossoms; illuminating pureness; melting body and mind, they became as one.

Qi connected to qi.

Meridians were harmonized with meridians.

Drops merged with drops.

For a very very very, long long long time; from eternity, to eternity, to eternity.

The White Tara told me, "In this human realm, not many know what desire really is."

"Who knows?"

"Grand Master Lu!"

The White Tara said, "Desire is medicine, not poison. Grand Master Lu is number one at understanding this."

The White Tara analyzed:

 Medicine has no leaks; it is only poison that leaks.

 Medicine is: Great happiness, brightness, emptiness.

 Poison is: Corrupt, obscene, has evil thoughts, hell.

 Attaining the four happiness and four emptiness is medicine.

 Damaging the body and performing bad deeds is poison.

 If it is the way I was born,

 Yet it also causes me to die then it is poison.

 If it is the way I was born,

 Yet it also allows me to live then it is medicine.

If you see the Buddha-nature because of it, it is medicine.
If you descend to hell because of it, it is poison.
The union of me and the White Tara unexpectedly entered a really profound meditation, the deepest form of meditation.

I knew that, no matter how I explained it, sentient beings in this saha world would not be able to understand me.

Who would know that, I Grand Master Lu understands "desire" better than anyone else. My level of practice is the highest in the world. I have surpassed "desire." I have achieved the "innate joy;" and I see the Buddha-nature.

"Forms are formless, formless are forms; forms do not differ from formless, formless do not differ from forms."

I know.

Worldly people do not know true "desire!" They only know how to conceive and bear sons and daughters, which is a low form of joy.

Only I really know "desire"! This is lamentable! In this regard, earthly people are ignorant!

Poem:

White Tara and a practitioner,
Meditate and worship profoundly.
Lotus flowers stand out from sludge.
The worldly mind transforms into Buddha mind.

The Jade Pond Golden Mother replied, "Where are misfortunes?"

Sheng-yen Lu

9. Jade Pond Pure Land

Further on, the Jade Hare led me to the Jade Pond Pure Land. This land was much more extraordinary. It was covered in mist with rose-colored clouds and five radiant colorful auspicious lights. One could hear the wonderful sounds of nature, the murmuring of flowing pure water; and experience exotic flowers, trees, and beautiful fragrant orchids. Colorful phoenix were everywhere, as were Night-blooming Cereus flowers, exquisite palaces, and seven precious jeweled pavilions, which liberated immortals.

I recognized the Jade Pond Pure Land.
I first met Qingluan, Shaoluan, and Xianluan.
Then, I met:
> Twelve Qingyao ladies;
> Twelve Jianggong ladies;
> Twelve Taisu ladies;
> Twelve Taixuan ladies;
> Twelve Huangsu ladies.

On arriving at the Jade Pond Pure Land, the Jade Hare no longer hid its identity. Shaking its body it immediately changed into a lady.

She wore a neon celestial cloth with an embroidered belt that waved in the breeze. The celestial cloth was pristine and dustless. Her waist was as delicate and thin as a willow.

Her eyebrows were like spring mountains and her eyes were like apricots. Her nose was like a goose's gallbladder; and a mouth as red as Cinnabar. Her ten pointing fingers were like spring bamboo shoots; her face as an apricot flower and cheeks like peach flowers.

Even Xishi could not compete with her beauty.

Even Chang-e would lose to her.

She was the celestial lady Dong Shuangcheng, the personal attendant of the Jade Pond Golden Mother, the great golden celestial ruler of the Jade Pond Pure Land.

The celestial lady Dong Shuangcheng led me to see the Jade Pond Golden Mother.

I don't dare to describe the Jade Pond Golden Mother, because the great golden divinity changes into thousands of forms and all are different.

Even if I were to describe them it would not be accurate.

Because the no-limit and no-form transformations are mystic, divine forms are extraordinary, yet are seldom known. Their bodily changes and illusive permutations are too mysterious to fathom. It is really quite difficult to accurately describe in writing what they truly look like.

I only can say that:
> She wore a phoenix crown;
> Held a divine peach;
> And grasped a celestial duster.

The Jade Pond Golden Mother opened her golden mouth and said, "Grand Master Lu, do you know why you have been guided here?"

I answered, "Know just one or two."

The Jade Pond Golden Mother said, "What is one? What is two?"

I replied, "One is to write about *The Divine Book*; two is for human beings to witness and become enlightened."

The Jade Pond Golden Mother asked, "By what Dharma?"

I answered, "By pondering inward."

The Jade Pond Golden Mother said, "I feel great compassion for the world's sentient beings, their endless incarnation cycles of life and death, chased by karma and enmity, and non-stop retribution. Grand Master Lu, do your best to finish the mission of saving sentient beings!"

I questioned, "How should I alleviate my own, Grand Master Lu's own misfortunes?"

The Jade Pond Golden Mother replied, "Where are misfortunes?"

These were the Jade Pond Golden Mother's "Zen words." Since I am enlightened, I understood immediately.

I accepted the Golden Mother's profound decrees and descended to return to the saha world!

Poem:

An illusory body visits the divine land.
Receives a decree and descends to return once more.
Inner thinking dharma that earns,
Thorough understanding of spirituality.
Teaches observance of the heart.

Grand Master Lu is endless and I have seen enough of these kinds of games. It does not bother me a bit.

Sheng-yen Lu

10. Seeing Fengfeng

In a previous chapter I wrote about "desire." It was based on my observations during deep meditation.

Perhaps someone would ask, "Grand Master Lu, do you see such events also happening here in the present world?"

I would laugh, "Certainly and often!"

Let me give an example!

I was consulted in a "divination room" by an attractive lady from a distant land who paid homage to me. She noticed that the attendants to my right and left had left the room.

She stood up after finishing the homage.

She then placed one hand on her head, shaking, and cried, "Grand Master Lu, please help me. I am too dizzy to hold myself up!"

I immediately put out a hand to support her.

But she hugged me tighter and then put her mouth to mine, almost becoming a Chinese character 呂. I tensed up and pushed her away.

She said to me, "You have missed out on my passion!"

Here is a second example:

A long haired voluptuous female approached me quietly asking, "Grand Master Lu, I heard that you have accomplished the Non-leaking Practice?"

I answered, "Correct."

She then passed me a note. On it, was written the room number of a hotel.

She said, "Let me help prove that you are not leaking!"

Before leaving, she looked back and gave me a seductive smile.

Of course, I tossed the paper into a trash can.

I followed this by saying "Sorry!" to the trash can.

***

In the third deep meditation I saw a shadow walking towards me. I was startled. It was "Fengfeng."

Fengfeng was a writer, and Buddhist writer. He had authored many books.

I met Fengfeng multiple times. Each time he published a new book he offered me a copy.

Fengfeng said to me, "I came today specially to inform you of one thing."

"What is it?"

Fengfeng responded, "One year, a woman from a far place asked me to treat an illness she had. She said she did not have much money on her. Being kind, I let her stay in my guest room. At night, she started groaning and I went into check on her."

"This female took my hand to her chest and said that her heart was beating very fast..."

Afterwards, Fengfeng said, "To my surprise, this female blackmailed me. To settle it, I spent a great amount of money."

I asked, "Why are you telling me this?"

Fengfeng became anxious, "Perhaps, this female is the same person who you encountered. She took advantage of me and thinks that she can do it again to you."

"Oh! I understand" I said. So that's what this was about.

I said to Fengfeng, "I was born with hard bones. Not to worry, I will be fine. She will not get a dime from me."

"But, what about your reputation?"

"I have no reputation." I said.

"But Grand Master Lu, your whole life will be finished!" Fengfeng warned.

I replied, "Grand Master Lu is endless and I have seen enough of these kinds of games. It does not bother me a bit."

"However, sentient beings mind!"

I answered, "Minding also equals not minding."

Fengfeng then responded, "You really don't mind?"

I responded, "My enlightenment is not fake!"

I then added, "In Tianning, Ruzhou, there was a Zen master named Ming. When the Zen master was about to enter nirvana, he said the following verse :

> *Casually pick up a wooden slip.*
> *Simultaneously put down the seat pad.*
> *Once clouds disperse, so does the water go away.*
> *Quiet sky and earth are void.*

I said, "Fengfeng, I truly appreciate that you told me this in person. You truly did not forget about our friendship."

Poem:

> *Once passed and bearing no shadow.*
> *A friend left a fragrance.*
> *Grateful the heart is for advice given to me.*
> *However, everything is empty, empty, empty.*

Realize that Dharmas are not constant. Buddha seeds begin from a karmic cause.

Sheng-yen Lu

11. Zen Discussion With Fengfeng

I met Fengfeng during meditation. I felt that the Fengfeng before his death and Fengfeng after his death were two different people.

Fengfeng before his death - readily expressed both his happiness and anger.

Fengfeng after his death - appeared to be a crane-riding eminent being.

Fengfeng asked me, "Sheng-yen Bodhisattva Grand Master Lu, I heard that you have been writing books about Zen Buddhism lately!"

I answered, "I studied the Pure Land Buddhism first and then Vajrayana Buddhism. In the middle of these studies I also learned the precepts. It is only recently that I have been writing books on Zen Buddhism."

Since Fengfeng liked to test me he continued, "In your opinion what is Zen?"

I replied, "Seeing it is better than hearing it!"

Fengfeng then asked, "So what is after seeing it?"

I answered, "That's how it is." (It's just like this. It's just like this.)

Fengfeng followed with yet another question, "What is meant by 'that's how it is'?"

I replied, "One doesn't even need to think about what is that's how it is."

Fengfeng then exclaimed, "Grand Master Lu, you truly are knowledgeable in Zen. No wonder you are amongst the most elite Buddhists. No one in the world can compete with you!"

I responded, "This Name and Form Zen essentially departs from Buddha-nature and is not the absolute. It should have been left alone but instead it changed and spread all around the world as it was differently interpreted by the four enlightened and six unenlightened beings."

Fengfeng nodded in agreement.

Fengfeng asked, "Having finished reading my book *Void Cloud*, do you have any comments about it?"

I responded, "Realize that Dharmas are not constant. Buddha seeds begin from a karmic cause."

Fengfeng listened and thought about it for a little while. He seemed to have grasped the weight of my words.

Fengfeng nodded his head and said, "I spent five years writing *Void Cloud*. I researched over one hundred books. It was difficult for me to write. It is amazing to me that in ten short characters you are able to summarize this large three-volume book thoroughly, which I racked my brain over for five years! I even totally isolated myself and refrained from contacting anyone."

Fengfeng continued, "Did you know that I was the one who told Professor Xie Bingying, the famous author of *Autobiography of a Female Soldier*, to take refuge in you?"

I answered, "Yes I remember that!"

Fengfeng said, "Well, did Professor Xie Bingying reach enlightenment?"

I answered, "Since she does not see the path yet, how can she reach the destination?"

Fengfeng could not help but sigh emotionally for a while after hearing what I said. Fengfeng mentioned that Professor Xie to him was like a teacher and friend. Their relationship was not shallow and they corresponded back and forth. It was a pity that she had not reached Buddhahood.

Poem:

> *Path to return is everywhere.*
> *Yet where is not the home.*
> *The path is already there.*
> *Once enlightened one feels at peace.*

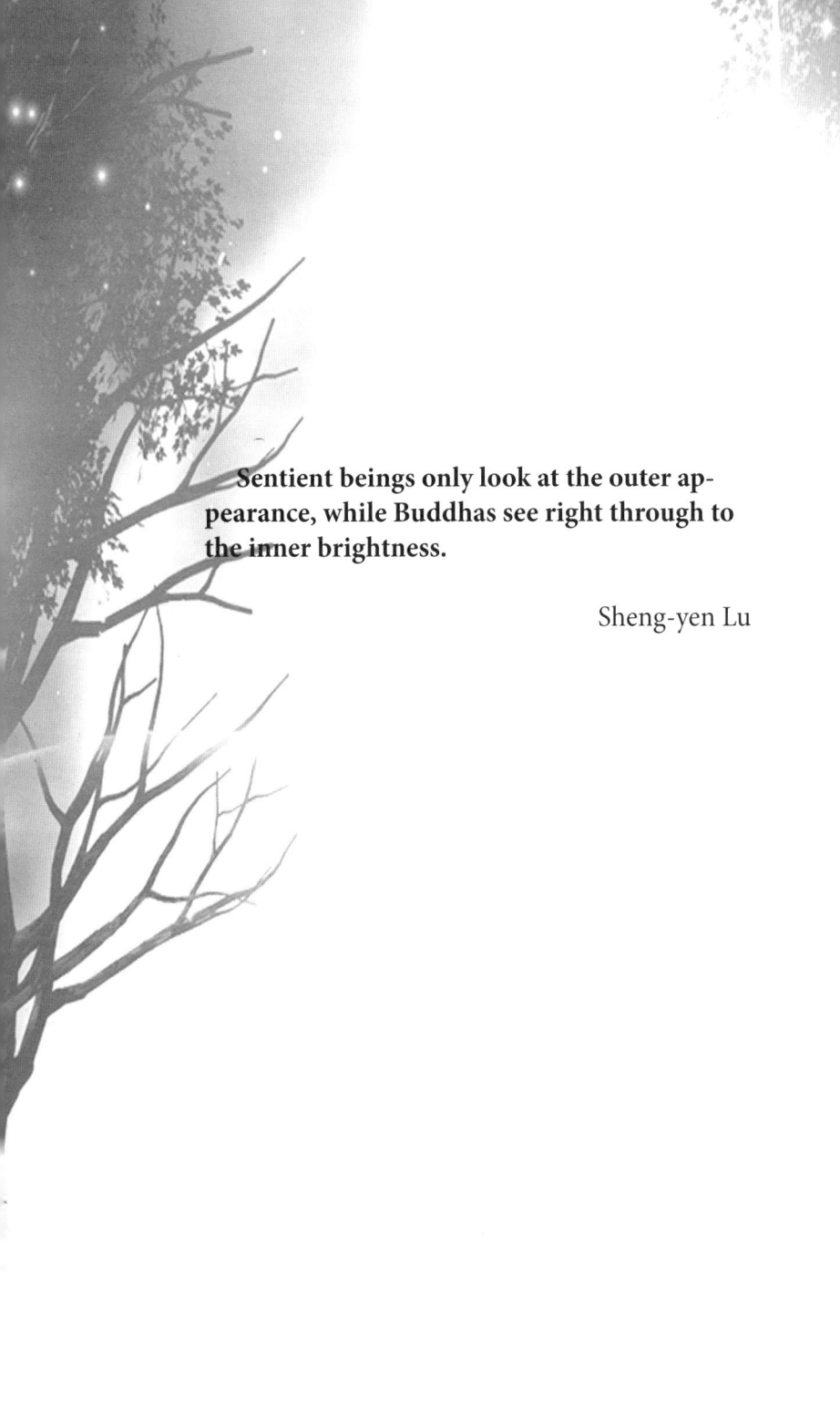

Sentient beings only look at the outer appearance, while Buddhas see right through to the inner brightness.

Sheng-yen Lu

12. Buddha King of the Era

I saw the layman Fengfeng during meditation. Fengfeng said to me, "Grand Master Lu, you are the Buddha king of this era!"

I laughed out loud and replied, "Nonsense!"

Fengfeng said "I overheard Sakyamuni Buddha telling this to Maitreya Bodhisattva at the Kaiyuan Temple in Tainan!"

I asked, "What are you saying?"

Fengfeng answered, "Sakyamuni Buddha said to Maitreya Bodhisattva that, in this world, one truly enlightened person is present. Grand Master Lu is the one. Only Grand Master Lu is qualified to be the king of the Buddhas. Maitreya Bodhisattva responded that this is indeed so. Grand Master Lu is seemingly unaffected and naturally spontaneous. He deserves it."

I said, "I am the founder of an evil religion in this era."

To this Fengfeng responded, "Then that must be you covering up your real identity!"

I added, "But I am a ravenous sex maniac."

Fengfeng objected and said, "Then it must be the Buddha decree that makes one not able to see the real you."

I replied with, "I wear gold and jade."

Fengfeng again responded, "It is that you cover up your inner self with your outer appearance."

I said, "Currently, Buddhism is very prosperous. The merit of the leader of each organization is as high as the sky. They all perform Dharma to large audiences. They are all cultivating eminent monks, acting virtuously, not viciously. These leaders are the true Dharma kings and Buddha kings!"

Fengfeng answered, "Sentient beings only look at the outer appearance, while Buddhas see right through to the inner brightness. One who can explain the meaning of the moon in the water and the flower in the mirror is slandered by sentient beings. Few would even recognize that such a person is indeed the true Buddha king!"

I asked, "What is the moon in the water? What is the flower in the mirror?"

Fengfeng answered, "In beef noodles, there is no beef. In the sun cake, there is no sun. In the moon cake, there is no moon, and in the wife cake, there is no wife. What do these also all refer to?"

I asked curiously, "How did you know?"

Fengfeng responded, "I participated in your Kalachakra ceremony in Linkou, Taiwan. I also took the empowerment. Anyone who understands these is the true Buddha king of this time!"

An "Oh!" escaped from me.

Then Fengfeng said, "The so-called founder of the evil religion, the ravenous sex maniac, who wears gold and jade is unexpectedly the Buddha king. To think that even wise people like me also almost missed you, not to mention blind sentient beings!"

I asked, "Fengfeng! What were you doing in the Kaiyuan Temple?"

Fengfeng replied, "I am the temple attendant and am responsible for watering the garden, sweeping, and taking care of the yard." As soon as he had finished talking, Fengfeng immediately transformed into an auspicious light and vanished!

Poem:

A real one is not revealed from outer appearances.
Revealed from outer appearance is not a real one.
It is necessary to hide one's identity.
Tell only major disciples.

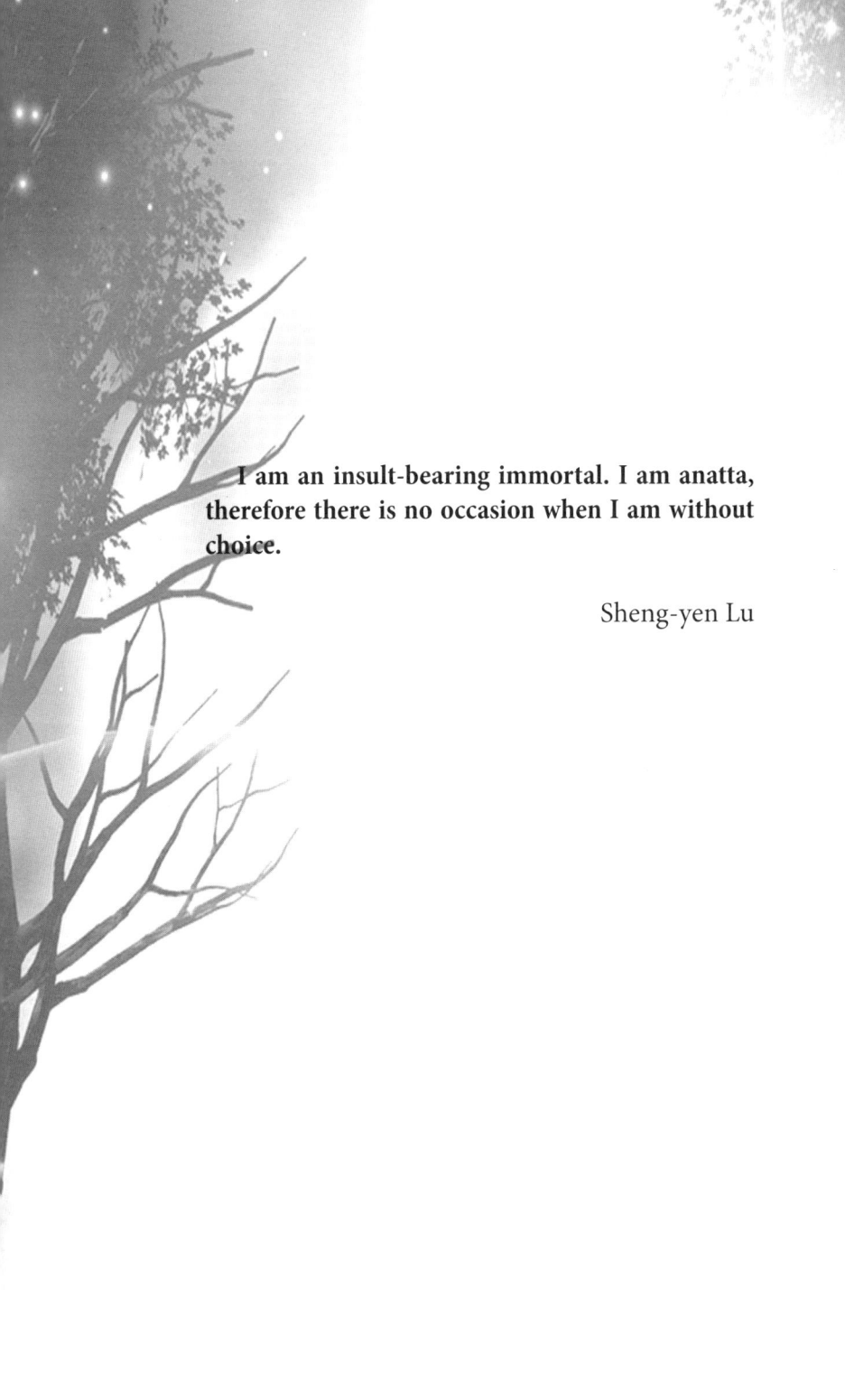

I am an insult-bearing immortal. I am anatta, therefore there is no occasion when I am without choice.

Sheng-yen Lu

13. Willy-Nilly Heaven

During my fourth experience of deep meditation, I was in a trance and so totally engrossed that I hardly remembered who I was. Before I knew it I had arrived in a new realm. I not only saw exotic grasses that were rich with fragrance but also indescribable immortal flowers. It was an exquisite place.

I looked at my surroundings. The ground was made of gold, there were magnificent jade palaces and finely decorated painted pillars and engraved eaves; it seemed quite obvious that this had to be a heavenly realm. However, the atmosphere felt gloomy.

I knew about heavenly realms:
>The Heavenly Desire Realm.
>The Heavenly Form Realm.
>The Heavenly Formless Realm.

I even wrote a book called *Staircase to the Heavens*, which described the twenty-eight heavenly realms. However, I still could not recognize which heavenly realm this was.

I was lost, so I looked inside my heart. *The Divine Book* then opened and there were three characters written, "Willy-Nilly Heaven".

However, this time, I was still confused. There is no Willy-Nilly

Heaven among the twenty-eight heavens. I only knew of a Willy-Nilly Bridge in the netherland, but never a Willy-Nilly Heaven?

While I hesitated, a practitioner approached in front of me.

The practitioner was singing:

> *See through that the good times in this human world,*
> *Will not last forever.*
> *That birth, aging, illness, and death are all sad.*
> *Pity those half-lacking ones' wish to fulfill their dreams.*
> *Come and lean on Willy-Nilly.*

I joined my palms and greeted the practitioner.

He greeted me in return.

I asked him, "Where are we? What is your name?"

The practitioner replied, "The name of the place is Willy-Nilly Heaven. And, I am a Willy-Nilly Practitioner."

I asked, "Why did I arrive at Willy-Nilly Heaven?"

The Willy-Nilly practitioner answered, "People living here are all willy-nilly people. Because of being willy-nilly they gather in Willy-Nilly heaven. As for you Grand Master Lu, you are in Willy-Nilly heaven because you must have experienced some willy-nilly matters."

I thought about it and agreed.

I asked the Willy-Nilly Practitioner, "Then why are you in Willy-Nilly Heaven?"

He answered, "I am Qu Yuan!"

As soon as I heard the name Qu Yuan, I was very surprised.

Qu Yuan said, "I am the genuine descendant of Zi Xia, the King of Chu Wu. Qu was my fiefdom. I took the inhabited area's name as my surname, I am Qu Yuan."

I thought of Qu Yuan's death by jumping into the Miluo River, of the dragon rowing boat, of the Dragon Boat Festival, and of eating steamed rice dumplings.

In addition, I thought about Qu Yuan's great work, *Li Sao*.
Deep in my heart I felt dejected.

Qu Yuan said, "You, Grand Master Lu, have a compassionate heart, but who will have mercy on you? You have no choice."

I answered, "You are correct that I have no other choice. However, I practice bearing humility. I am an insult-bearing immortal. I am anatta, therefore there is no occasion when I am without choice."

Poem:

Willy-Nilly also exists as a heaven.
Justice is not in the human heart.
If you want to find discontented impartial people,
All are here being small immortals.

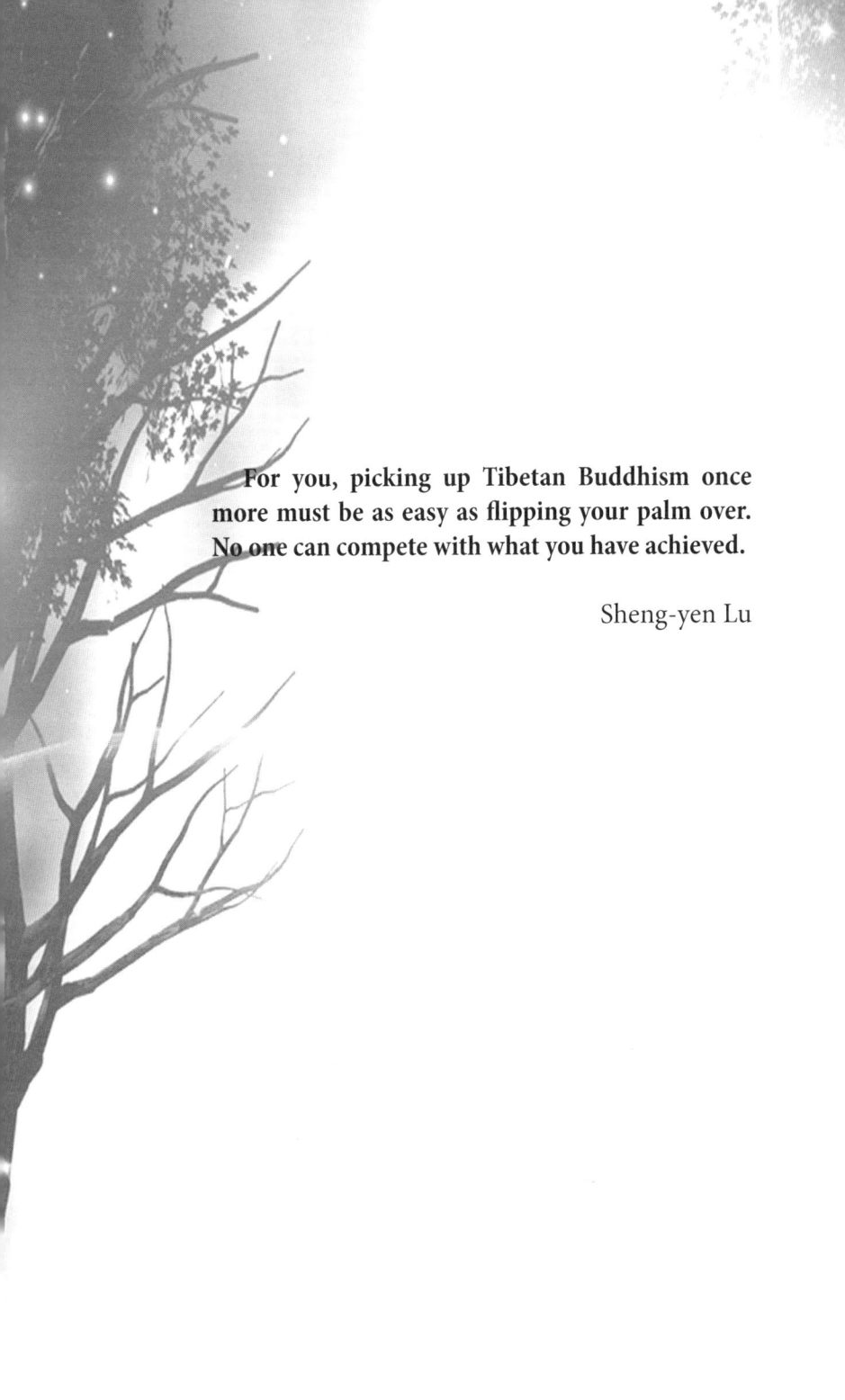

For you, picking up Tibetan Buddhism once more must be as easy as flipping your palm over. No one can compete with what you have achieved.

Sheng-yen Lu

14. Princess Wencheng

I arrived in the Willy-Nilly Heaven during deep meditation. There I met with the renown patriotic poet Qu Yuan.
I asked Qu Yuan, "Who else lives in Willy-Nilly Heaven?"
Instead of responding to my question Qu Yuan asked me, "So you study Tibetan Buddhism! I heard that you have achieved great things. Is this correct?"
"Yes it is. However, the key points of Tibetan Buddhism are renunciation, Bodhicitta, and the true view of Madhyamaka."
Qu Yuan said, "Let me present to you someone special. You will never guess who."
"Who is it?" I asked.
Qu Yuan answered, "Princess Wencheng."
"Princess Wencheng! Do you mean the one who married Songzain Gambo, the thirty-second Zanpu of Turfan?"
"Yes, precisely."
Now I was totally dumbfounded. Princess Wencheng was a daughter of the imperial clan of Emperor Taitsung of the Tang Dynasty. In the fifteenth Zhenguan year of Tang (641 AD), she entered Tibet and married the king of Turfan. Princess Wencheng was a talented wom-

an. She introduced to Turfan the science and technology of textile weaving, architecture, metallurgy, medicine, the almanac, and so on.

Songzain Gambo already had a wife, Princess Chezun. She was the daughter of the Nepalese King Zhouwang, and married Songzain Gambo in 634 AD.

I asked Qu Yuan, "Why is Princess Wencheng in the Willy-Nilly Heaven?"

Qu Yuan answered, "For Princess Wencheng, leaving Changan was not her decision. Living in the foreign land offered no way out for her. The Turfan king's death from illness a few years after their marriage was not intentional. Not being able to return to the Tang Dynasty was not her choice. Also..."

I was speechless.

Qu Yuan recited:

> *Weeping from homesickness,*
> *While viewing from the summit;*
> *A thousand mile east wind,*
> *Makes a dream seem remote.*

I arrived at the palace of Princess Wencheng with Qu Yuan. It was a brilliantly colored vermilion home with golden paved floors, and had the snow white sparkling elegant windows of a jade palace. It was indeed a heavenly realm quite different from the human world.

Princess Wencheng's hair, swept up into a chignon, was decorated with pearls and jade, gently swirling lotus sleeves; gracefully waving feather garments; exquisite looking as spring blossoms and enticing as the autumn moon.

I smelled the lingering essence of a delicate aroma and wondered what it was?

Just then Princess Wencheng spoke, "This incense is a unique product from Tibet. It is made from the extract of an exotic wood and burned with tree oil. I am entitled to this incense for ten thousand years."

I said to Princess Wencheng, "Back then you built the Jokhang Monastery, which was flooded several times. Since you understood geomancy, knowing that Tibet was a supine Raksasi whose heart was a lake, you leveled the lake and constructed the temple there. It subsequently eradicated calamities and drove away evil."

Princess Wencheng smiled with indifference and said, "Grand Master Lu, have you forgotten your previous lives?"

I answered, "How could I forget them?"

Princess Wencheng smiled, "You were a great patriarch of Tibetan Buddhism. For you, picking up Tibetan Buddhism once more must be as easy as flipping your palm over. No one can compete with what you have achieved."

Princess Wencheng said, "Today, only I know this, besides the Buddha, Padmasambhava, and Vajrasattva. As to ordinary people, how could they know? This is also no way out for you!"

I said, "Heaven! Heaven!"

Poem:

The exotic land is not ordinary.
One can end up there like a flying goose.
What is originally willy-nilly.
Is still an endless melody.

I realized deeply that, to be an achiever, one must possess endless stamina and completely devote body and heart to the world's sentient beings.

Sheng-yen Lu

15. Encountering Bi Gan

During the fourth deep meditation, I arrived at the Willy-Nilly Heaven and met Qu Yuan and then Princess Wencheng.
After leaving the Remote Palace of Dreams (Princess Wencheng's palace) I unexpectedly encountered Bi Gan.
First listen to my poem:

> *For what are wealthy and prominent?*
> *One cannot disobey the Emperor's order.*
> *Pity those with empty hearts,*
> *Transformed into soaring souls.*

***

Encountering Bi Gan in the Willy-Nilly Heaven shook me up greatly.
This Bi Gan was none other than Prime Minister Bi Gan of King Chou of the Shan Dynasty.
Historical facts recorded in the *Annals of Yin* stated that: "King Chou was constantly promiscuous and refused to listen to the repeat-

ed admonishments from his officials. Eventually the officials decided to meet with the imperial tutor and assistant imperial tutor for a remonstration.

Bi Gan said, "As an official of the emperor, I shall fight this with my life." Bi Gan strongly pleaded with King Chou.

But King Chou responded angrily with an order: "I heard that the heart of a saint has seven orifices. So let us dissect Bi Gan's heart and observe it's orifices!"

How I knew about Bi Gan was because Jiang Ziya was the earliest ancestor of the Lu clan and Lu is a branch of the Jiang family. Jiang Ziya and Bi Gan were from the same dynasty.

Historical records from the The Clan of Qi in the *Shihchi* wrote that: "The great Wang Lushang was also known as Jiang Shang. His ancestor had assisted Yu recover from a flood and was rewarded with the surname Lu. By adopting the awarded last name, Lu Shang had become Jiang Shang. But Jiang Ziya was destitute; he hooked Zhou Xibo by fishing."

In the *Shihchi*, it is written :"Jiang Shang was a civil and military master."

***

There had to be a good reason for Bi Gan to be in the Willy-Nilly Heaven. I knew that in Taiwan, Qu Yuan has a temple dedicated to him: Qu Yuan Temple. People address him as the Water Celestial King. However, I have no idea whether anyone worshiped Bi Gan.

Bi Gan saw me and asked, "Grand Master Lu! Why are you in the Willy-Nilly Heaven?"

I answered, "I am here because I am an insult-bearing immortal who endures slander!"

Bi Gan laughed out loud, "If Grand Master Lu was slandered by people for a minor reason yet already calls himself an insult-bearing immortal; then, what sort of immortal must I be ?"

I blushed and felt quite ashamed after listening to him. Yes, was it such a big deal that I was slandered. Being slandered is not painful or itchy. It does not require me to sacrifice my life or give my heart. What kind of shame-enduring immortal is that?

Bi Gan asked me, "Can you sacrifice your heart?"

I answered, "The Bodhicitta of Vajrayana buddhism means four immeasurable vows: loving-kindness, compassion, joy, and equanimity. I will sacrifice whenever it is needed."

Bi Gan asked me, "You will give up your life too?"

I answered, "I took a solemn vow that I would have my body shattered and my bones crushed to save sentient beings. Who will be in hell if I myself will not enter it. Wouldn't this be the same as giving myself up?"

Bi Gan responded, "This is close. Bear what is hard to bear, accomplish what is difficult to perform, and do not withdraw when sacrifice is needed. This is what Willy-Nilly is all about. What can you do to me now? Ha ha!"

After a lesson from Bi Gan, I realized deeply that, to be an achiever, one must possess endless stamina and completely devote body and heart to the world's sentient beings.

Poem:

Bi Gan gave his heart and died.
He is entitled to be a Willy-Nilly being.
Those who pursue fame and fortune.
Have been detested since the beginning of time.

This person was quite unusual; he was a strange person, a sage, virtuous person, an unconventional person, and an eccentric.

Sheng-yen Lu

16. The Stranger Xu You

Once again while in deep meditation I arrived at the Willy-Nilly Heaven. Qu Yuan, again took me to meet someone.

This person was quite unusual; he was a strange person, a sage, virtuous person, an unconventional person, and an eccentric.

He rarely spoke, perhaps one and a half sentences every six months or year. When he did speak, it would only be, "I have nothing to say!" or, "What is there to say!"

This person meditated every day but he did not read sutras. Someone offered him the Buddhist sutras but he did not look at them or turn any pages as if he had no interest.

One day, when at last he finally opened his mouth to speak, he said, "I am illiterate."

"But illiterates can still learn!" I responded.

He answered, "Why be literate?"

Immortals in the Willy-Nilly Heaven all knew about this odd mute person.

Someone wrote the word "heart" on his front door, his window, and his wall.

This odd person said nothing. He simply washed all the "hearts" off with water. A year went by before he said:, "A door is a door. A window is a window. A wall is a wall. A heart is superfluous here."

This odd strange person had no friends nor did he see anyone. There were people around him but he ignored them, treating them as if he did not see them. Some even greeted him, "Long time no see! How've you been?"

But he never replied.

If he did answer, his response was, "Same."

I was curious and extremely interested to find out more about this personality in the Willy-Nilly Heaven. Qu Yuan led me over to meet him.

I said to him, "I am Grand Master Lu."

He did not respond.

I said, "Where would you tend a cow if it is in an area without grass?" (Zen talk.)

Unresponsively, he raised his head and look at me once, simply pointing his finger nowhere in particular.

I asked, "Who are you?"

Again he did not reply.

I asked, "There is a saying about emptying all five senses. Have you emptied all five of your senses?"

Yet he still did not answer; he only raised his head looking once more at me.

Not willing to give it up I asked again, "What is the awakened mind?"

This time around he opened his mouth. He replied, "One has a guest and does not care to reply." (A greatly profound purport.)

I followed with another question, "What do you eat?"

He answered, "It is not edible!"(This too has a greatly profound purport.)

Poem:

"The Divine Book" I consulted.
Declares that it is Xu You.
Strangely, he is an odd person.
He desires nothing.

Perseverance first, perception first, world creation first; save sentient beings generation after generation.

Sheng-yen Lu

17. Fond of the Willy-Nilly Heaven

I remember when I visited the heavenly realms, I stayed in the Wondrous Milky Way for a long time. Immortals there were quite peaceful and comfortable. I would very much like to return to the Wondrous Milky Way. The immortals there are waiting for me to return!

However, in the Willy-Nilly Heaven I met Qu Yuan, Princess Wencheng, Bi Gan, Xu You, ...

I began to like the Willy-Nilly Heaven because I realized that all the residents were "righteous" humans. The character of righteousness is what I have yearned for.

I asked, "Do Yao, Shun, and Yu live here in this homeland?"

Qu Yuan answered, "No."

I asked, "Do Confucius, Mencius, Zigong, Ziyou, and so on live in this homeland?"

Qu Yuan answered, "No."

I asked, "Do Fuxi, Nuwa, Yuchao, Suiren, Shennong, and so on live in this homeland?"

Qu Yuan answered, "No."

All the figures I asked about were sages and worthy people from former times. All achieved great things. They were also all righteous human beings. But why are none of them in the Willy-Nilly Heaven? This puzzled me?

Qu Yuan saw my confusion and said to me, "The righteous people in the Willy-Nilly Heaven all had grievances, or failed to achieve their goals in some way. Because of that it is called the Willy-Nilly Heaven!"

I said, "I like the Willy-Nilly Heaven. I would like this to be my homeland. I shall stay in the Willy-Nilly Heaven and not return to the saha world."

Qu Yuan said, "Certainly your experiences qualify you to remain in the Willy-Nilly Heaven. However, your vows allow you to go far, plus you are above grievances. You are overqualified for the Willy-Nilly Heaven. Do not stay in the Willy-Nilly Heaven any longer. You had better leave!"

I asked Qu Yuan, "But you reside here. Where should I return to?"

Qu Yuan replied, "Why not consult *The Divine Book.*"

I looked into my heart to consult *The Divine Book*. Therein appeared two characters, "Human World."

Followed by a few lines of small characters, that read: "Perseverance first, perception first, world creation first; save sentient beings generation after generation."

I almost passed out after reading this.

I then said, "My soul is ready to return, but where is my homeland?"

Qu Yuan said, "Live nowhere."

I answered, "Therefore I cannot stop here at the Willy-Nilly Heaven!"

Qu Yuan responded, "You must turn the Tathagata Dharma wheel!" In addition, "Dharmas originate from within. One must stay in a quiescent phase. These, you must be aware of."

As soon as I heard these sentences I came out of meditation!

Poem:

Often descend to the human world.
Where ease and joy cannot pursue.
Realize the Spring, Summer, Fall, and Winter.
Flies the bustling vermillion dust clouds.
(This truly is willy-nilly!)

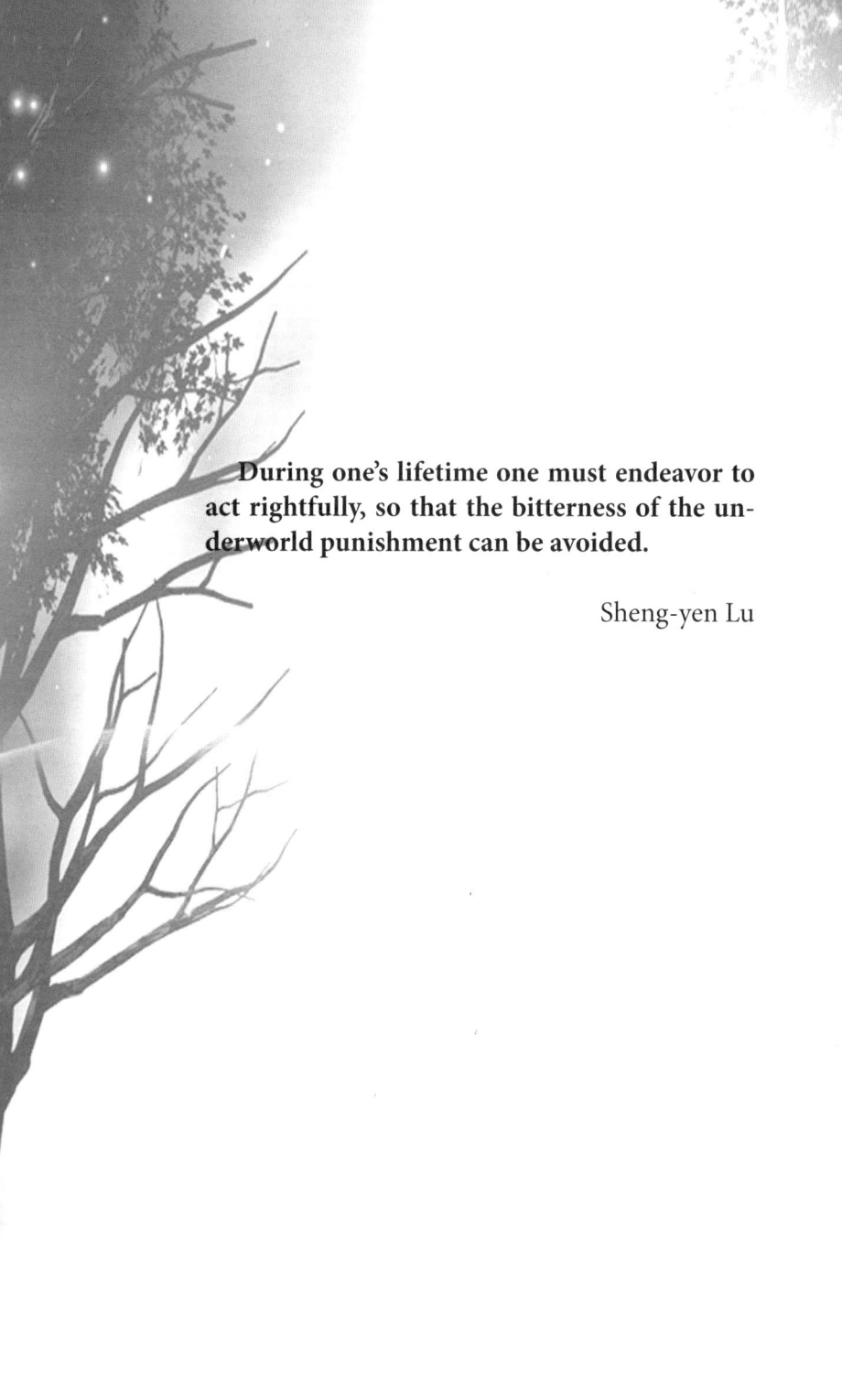

During one's lifetime one must endeavor to act rightfully, so that the bitterness of the underworld punishment can be avoided.

Sheng-yen Lu

18. Senlou Palace

During my fifth round of profound meditation, out in my illusory body, I felt as light as a feather. Vaguely and boundlessly, it was as if I was riding on clouds and sailing in the mist. It also seemed as if I was a waft of light breeze.

Drifting then landing, I saw a city. Above the city was written "Yin Yang Boundary Senluo Palace."

While I was still wondering outside Senluo Palace, three characters appeared. One was an impure elderly taoist. The other two were females with upright willowy eyebrows and apricot-shaped eyes that shone fiercely.

As soon as these three saw me, they lit up with anger and yelled, "Grand Master Lu arrived just at the right time. Since we are seeing you today, we must take your dog-life."

I asked, "Who are you three?"

The three did not answer. The impure old taoist raised his duster. A "Cloud Penetration Arrow" shot towards my face.

And as for the two females, one made a move of "Overturn the Heavens," and the other, "Heavenly Axe." All of them attacked me from above my head at once.

Ten thousand blue-green lights became airborne mixing with the sound of wind and thunder; they wanted to take my life.

Without any time to think, I desperately chanted the "Armor Protection Mantra." Vajrasattva appeared, transformed into a blue light, and covered my whole body.

Outside the blue light the "Cloud Penetration Arrow" could not get through.

Held by the blue light the "Overturns the Heavens" on top of my head could not move downwards.

The blue light also blocked the slash of "Heavenly Axe".

I became like a "golden bell-shaped hood" unscathed by any knives and guns.

I consulted *The Divine Book* which revealed three characters, "Jealousy, Affection, Love".

At that very moment I did not dare to think any more. I could only consider how to repel these enemies. I began to chant the Nine Syllable Mantra - *Lin, bing, dou, zhe, jie, zhen, lie, zai, qian* [literal translation: Presence, Soldier, Fight, Troops, All, Disposition, Row, At, Front].

This then caused the genuine samadhi fire to be emitted .

Immediately, the "Cloud Penetration Arrow" was burned.

The "Overturns the Heavens" movement was burned to ash.

And the "Heavenly Axe" melted into liquid iron.

Once the impure old taoist and two females saw their majestic weapons broken, they withdrew back into the Senluo Palace disappearing without a trace.

I pursued them into the Senluo Palace and only saw King Yama and the underworld judges. Below them were ox-head and horse-face ghost messengers. King Yama was busy trying many criminals who were imprisoned with cangues and fettered. They had all committed sins while living. It was quite pitiful!

There were disobedient, and unloyal, unfilial children.

Some who stole, robbed, swindled, and deceived.
Others who committed rape and murder, or improper sex.
Were dishonest.
Unfair and illegal.
That greedily accepted bribes.
Set things on fire to vent their hatred.
Made false accusations and slandered...

King Yama was indeed busily engaged. Seeing what happened there, I felt: During one's lifetime one must endeavor to act rightfully, so that the bitterness of the underworld punishment can be avoided.

Once King Yama had finished his sentencing, he raised his head and was very happy to see me, "Grand Master Lu! When did your distinguished presence arrive?"

King Yama stepped down the stairway to welcome me.

I said, "King Yama, did you see an old taoist and two females? They dodged into the Senluo Palace and disappeared!" I described the three.

King Yama told the underworld judges, "Search for these three immediately."

The judges replied that the three did not exist.

King Yama said, "But Grand Master Lu said that these were the three. How can they possibly not exist?" King Yama got out the *Book of Life and Death*. After consulting it he saw three characters written "Jealousy, Affection, Love."

King Yama said, "I get it. This was simply your imagination. Jealousy was the impure old taoist. The old fellow was jealous of your talent and worldwide reputation. He long ago wanted to harm you. Affection was one of the females. She had affection for Grand Master Lu but after receiving no response from you, she also wanted to hurt you. And Love was the other female. She loved you but you only love sentient beings. Her inability to love you turned her love into hatred. She wanted to sink the boat with the "Heavenly Axe" and die together with you.

"How did they disappear?"

King Yama said, "Because you are implicated in the three matters of jealousy, affection, and love, they appeared following your thought while you were thinking slightly. However, none of the three are in the palace. I will deal with them when they return here in the future."

I asked King Yama, "Do you see any of my disciples being degenerated here?"

King Yama answered, "Yes."

"How will you deal with them?"

King Yama answered, "As long as they remember Grand Master Lu, chant the heart mantra of Grand Master Lu, take refuge, accept empowerment, become a monk, or recite a mantra, they will ascend to the court of the heaven. But, if they violate the vows, are filled with betrayal or slander, only then will they descend to hell!"

Poem:

Cause and effect are like god.
One must not have wrong thoughts.
A karma is repaid with karma.
It is not at all ambiguous.

19. Five Direction Deities of Plague

During my fifth round of deep meditation, I entered the underworld and there I met with King Yama.

While we were conversing in the Senluo Palace, there was a sudden tumultuous raucous. Within a moments thousands of people crashed in.

King Yama asked a ghost messenger, "What is going on?"

The ghost messenger answered, "A plague has infected the human world and many people have suddenly died."

King Yama said to me, "Grand Master Lu, do you know how big your merit is?"

I answered, "I do not know."

King Yama said, "Your merit is as high as the sky!"

I was somewhat bewildered. What does this mean as high as the sky? I had never thought about it.

King Yama said, "One year ago, Lord Indra ordered all Five Direction Deities of Plague to descend to the human world at the same time. The world was supposed to encounter the biggest calamity in several hundred years. The Five Direction Deities of Plague were not trivial; they planned to put more than half of humanity away and even spread the epidemic to the whole world. The entire world was terrified."

King Yama continued, "At that time, you were in a retreat. In order to rescue all living beings, you ascended to the celestial realm of the Jade Pond and obtained the divine bag from the Golden Mother of the Jade Pond. You then returned to the saha world and used the bag to restrain the Five Direction Deities of Plague. The huge plague which was originally intended to destroy all of humanity disappeared abruptly. It was supposed to be a big human catastrophe but you saved all in one shot."

I said, "That was true, however, I thought it was only a small plague and that humanity was able to control it, not the merit of the divine bag from the Golden Mother of the Jade Pond. Was it really meant to be a big human catastrophe?"

King Yama answered, "Lord Indra wanted to destroy more than half of humanity before he was willing to stop, but you accidentally rescued humanity. To pay respect to the face of the Golden Mother of the Jade Pond, Lord Indra had to suppress the catastrophe. Did you realize that you had, without warning, put away the Five Direction Deities of Plague all at once?"

My hair stood on end. It was truly hard for me to believe.

King Yama said, "It was because of your existence in the saha world and your the teaching of your disciples to chant the Great Disaster Eradication Mantra. Having the celestial bag from the Golden Mother of the Jade Pond and the Great Disaster Eradication Mantra dissolved this human crisis."

My mouth hung open in astonishment; I was dumbfounded.

I asked the King, "Why did Lord Indra want to destroy humanity?"

King Yama answered, "Lord Indra saw the hearts of humanity becoming increasingly selfish, stupid, foul-smelling, and filthy. Both acts and thoughts were sinful. People no longer felt any shame especially in killing, stealing, committing incest or perverse sexual relations, and lying. Lord Indra was angry and therefore ordered the disaster!"

I said, "In the human world, there are still many saints and sages who practice compassionate teaching."

King Yama responded, "Only a few."

I said that, "Besides, the widespread promotion of Buddhism that can save humanity!"

King Yama said, "Superficially."

"Why superficially?" I asked.

"Fame and fortune merely!" King Yama answered. He added, "Between heaven and earth, there are few that are enlightened in this large human world but you are one of them. However, it is a great pity that, regardless of how diligently you have done your duty, humanity does not see it. In addition, infamy only increases not decreases. When a genuinely enlightened Buddha has been slandered and insulted by the people, even ten great King Yamas would be unable to avoid showing anger!"

I laughed, "But it has been this way since the beginning."

King Yama said, "However, why does humanity have to be so blind by blindly flattering hypocrites yet defaming the enlightened with profanity?"

Responding I said, "After all bear in mind that in the human world, the enlightened ones such as Buddha are as few as stars in the daytime, while the unenlightened are as abundant as grains of sand in the Ganges. Think about it. It is simply how it is. Why be angry?"

King Yama nodded, "No wonder only a few ascend to heaven while many descend into hell more than carps passing through the river."

I asked, "When will this human world plague cease?"

King Yama answered, "It will never end as long as humanity does not have a virtuous mind."

I then asked, "Will the Five Direction Deities of Plague ever again descend together?"

King Yama answered, "As long as Grand Master Lu is in samsara, the Five Direction Deities of Plague who fear you naturally will not come down again. However, as soon as you return to heaven, the Five Direction Deities of Plague will inevitably descend and humanity will be completely annihilated at that time."

Poem:

People's hearts are like vipers.
Lord Indra rages furiously.
Pray to the great saints and sages.
Forever live in the mundane world.

20. The Lotus Flower Family

During one of my deep meditations, King Yama and I were talking about the good old days. King Yama showed me the largest tourist attraction in hell. "Tourist attraction" is a modern term.

It was the famous "karmic mirror station" of hell. There is said to be only one karmic mirror station but in fact, there are five of them. These five include the:
- Past station
- Current station
- Future station
- Prediction station
- Local scenery station

I met up with Cakravartin. He was extremely respectful towards me.

Cakravartin asked, "Grand Master Lu, what do you want to look at?"

I answered, "I would like to look at the lotus flower family."

Cakravartin first opened the "eastern window." After a glance, it was clear that it was the world of the True Buddha lotus flowers, red, yellow, indigo, white, orange, green, ... The assorted lotus flowers had bloomed and were open. A young lad was on every lotus flower, eighteen large flowers, five hundred medium flowers, and thousands and thousands of small flowers. They were all filled with auspicious light and looked very attractive.

Cakravartin next opened the "southern window." I looked out and saw the shrine of the Southern Mountain Retreat where I live. I saw myself sitting cross-legged in front of the shrine and meditating. My eyes were closed and I was breathing lightly. It was a scene of the illusory body of Grand Master Lu being out.

Cakravartin then opened the "west window." There I saw the True Buddha lotus flower family prospering. Tons of lotus flowers were blossoming producing abundant rainbow colors. More then a million, even trillions of sentient beings were being saved. It was immeasurable. My innermost feelings were quite gratified.

Cakravartin then opened the "north window." This time the scene took me by surprise, because I saw only fifteen of eighteen large lotus flowers. Where had the remaining three gone? What I could see were only the dead twigs and withered leaves. The lotus flowers had wilted. The sight was pitiful.

I asked King Yama, "Eighteen large lotus flowers - why do only fifteen remain?"

King Yama answered, "Eighteen large lotus flowers descended into this world but three were abducted by the world. Fame and fortune clouded the mind. These three big lotus flowers have been in hell; they cannot return to the heaven realm and will transmigrate and suffer endlessly."

I cried loudly.

King Yama continued, "This saha world is an imaginary palace, where even large Bodhisattvas can easily lose their self-nature and fall into the morass. There are already many big Bodhisattvas imprisoned here in hell. The lotus flower clan of Grand Master Lu are the most precious. Losing only three big lotus flowers is actually very fortu-

nate."
King Yama said:
"The Asura race, has been annihilated.
The Demon race, has only one person remaining.
Nine Sunlight races have lost six generals.
The Four Devas race, has lost even more.
Heaven race has lost half.
The Lotus Flower race, lost three large lotus flowers..."
I listened. It was really shocking! At the same time, I was deeply saddened for these three big lotus flowers.
I asked, "How can they be rescued?"
King Yama answered, "Only if awakened."
I said, "I am under illusion and know it is merely an illusion. I did my best and understood the illusion, and did my best and exited the illusion."
King Yama said, "This is undeceivable willpower!" Followed by, "Being undeceiving is a truly enlightened one."
I said, "Presently, how are the three big lotus flowers?"
King Yama said, "Take illusion as reality, self deceiving."
Then Cakravartin opened central "local scenery station." I took a look at it. It was the "Buddha" that was in there.
(Amitabha Buddha)
The body of the Amitabha Buddha is golden, with a nice appearance and radiance that are incomparable.
Bright rays shine around five Mount Merus. Pure violet eyes are as the four large oceans.
Trillions of Buddhas have been transformed from the illumination. Transformed Bodhisattvas are also infinite.
Saving sentient beings with forty-eight vows, and taking all nine levels to the other end.
This Amitabha Tathagata is the Immeasurable Light Tathagata, Boundless Light Tathagata, Unobstructive Light Tathagata, Unreflec-

tive Light Tathagata, Brilliant Light Tathagata, Pure Light Tathagata, Delighted Light Tathagata, Wisdom Light Tathagata, Unceasing Light Tathagata, Unthinkable Light Tathagata, Nameless Light Tathagata, Ultra Moon and Sun Light Tathagata.

Only bliss exists in the pure land of Amitabha Buddha. Also existing are, four-treasure seven tiers of railings, seven layers of netting, seven rows of trees, seven-treasure pond, eight merit water, seven-treasure pavilions, large, medium and small lotus flowers, subtle, wonderful, fragrant, pure, heavenly melodies, ...

King Yama said, "This is Grand Master Lu!"

I was silent.

I certainly knew who I am.

Poem:

Brilliant light is in the West.
Banquets are near the pure pond.
Bliss is the most suitable.
Centuries are long as so.

21. Divination of Future Fortune or Not

In Vajrayana Buddhism, there is a goddess who is most famous for her ability to divine the future. The goddess holds a place in the heavenly realms. This great goddess is Mahasri.

Mahasri is also called Laksmi. Her father is Taksaka; her mother, Hariti; and she is the younger sister of Vaiśramana.

The *Golden Light Sutra* records: "The Realm of Laksmi".

The *Most Distinctive King Sutra* records: "The Realm of Great Mahasri".

Both *The Sutra of Buddha Discourses Regarding the Twelve Names of Mahasri* and *The Sutra of Twelve Names and One Hundred and Eight Names of Mahasri in the Immaculate Mahayana* have records of Mahasri.

The great Mahasri has, "An upright body of reddish-white, wearing pearl and jade bracelets and earrings, celestial clothes and a bejeweled crown; holds a wish-fulfilling pearl in her left hand, offers the dauntless mudra with the right hand, and stands on a lotus flower bed."

I have a statue of her in the Southern Mountain Retreat for me to worship. I chant the mantra of the Mahasri every day, "*Om, ma-ha-si-lee-yeh, so-ha.*"

***

I was meeting with King Yama, the Lord of the netherworld.

I asked King Yama, "Although I already know that my origin is Amitabha Buddha, I still very much want to know if my own future is going to be good or bad!"

King Yama laughed loudly, "Why don't you ask Mahasri. Her divination of good or bad luck is known to be the best."

King Yama thought for a second and continued, "Grand Master Lu, you forget something! You divine for others yourself, don't you? Why not divine your own future?"

I could not help but laugh. Of course, I am the number one divinator Lu Sheng-yen. In the old days, I divined for three hundred people a day; I was able to foretell good and bad, fortunate and unfortunate futures immediately. It was wondrous.

And now, I wanted to know my own future's fortune, but didn't divine for myself; instead I wanted to have Mahasri do it for me! How big a joke was that?

I asked King Yama, "I don't want to divine any more. I only want to find out the future of the three large lotus flowers?"

(These three big lotus flowers are my biggest concern.)

King Yama said, "Not to worry! Do you know who was previously in hell?"

"Who?"

"Shakyamuni Buddha was imprisoned in hell. Moreover, he transmigrated to animal realms. He was an elephant king, deer king, and monkey king. Shakyamuni Buddha violated the precepts by killing and conducting improper sex. Many Bodhisattvas also have gone to hell, including monks at Four-Meditation Heavens. Therefore, you don't need to too worry about the three large lotus flowers of your lotus flower race."

I responded "Of course. Of course!"

King Yama said, "You wanted to see your own future. Don't you have *The Divine Book* gifted from Maitreya Bodhisattva? Why not consult it?"

"This really is one word that awakens a dreaming person!"

I did consult *The Divine Book* and was stunned by the passage, "All but blank."

Blank, blank, blank, blank, blank.

I completely understood now.

King Yama smiled. King Yama then told me a story:

"In the past, there was a monk who was fond of reading the *Lotus Sutra* (*Ingenious Dharma Lotus Flower Sutra*). When reading that 'The essence of all Dharmas has been the same from the beginning of time. It is perpetually in a quiescent formless state,' he suddenly hesitated.

The Buddhist priest pondered deeply about the fact that 'The essence of all Dharmas has been the same from the beginning of time. It is perpetually in a quiescent formless state.' Regardless of whether walking, living, sitting, or lying, he was contemplating these words. However, despite his restless thoughts, he was still clueless.

Suddenly, he was awakened on hearing yellow orioles singing on branches heralding the arrival of Spring.

The Buddhist priest then wrote a verse:

> *The essence of all Dharmas,*
> *Has been the same from the beginning of time.*
> *It is perpetually in a quiescent formless state.*
> *On the arrival of the spring, a hundred flowers bloom,*
> *Yellow orioles sing on willow trees.*

King Yama said to me, "You consulted *The Divine Book* and the result was blank. Do you comprehend this? What is lucky? What is ominous?"

I answered, "I understand! I understand!"

King Yama said, "Today's worldly slander is nothing but the singing of orioles on tree branches!"

I answered, "Yes I understand! I understand!"

"Grand Master Lu, take a look who King Yama is?"

I looked at him and was very surprised. King Yama was actually transformed from Ksitigarbha Bodhisattva.

"How can it be you?"

"Although appearance is universal, seeing can be biased" said Ksitigarbha Bodhisattva said.

Poem:

Does luck or misfortune ever truly exist.
They are actually blank.
All dharma exists originally.
One can observe by looking within.

22. The Patriarch Bodhidharma Said as Such

In my sixth round of deep meditation, the Water Heaven unexpectedly appeared. It was a beautiful, crystal bright, and transparent city.
It truly:
    Resembled heaven yet was not heaven,
    Resembled earth yet was not earth.
The Water Heaven was an inverted image of the entire realm of heaven. The Water Heaven encompassed the beauty of all heavenly realms. It was so beautiful that it could not be described with any beautiful word. Although water was in the name the Water Heaven, it was not real water.
The boundary protection of the Water Heaven was the greatest of all. Very few could enter inside the protected Water Heaven boundary, as it was flawless.
Even the Dragon King is unable to enter the Water Heaven. I was able to enter the Water Heaven because I am a Buddha. Only those whose practice has reached the supreme level can enter.
I was already in the illusory body.
Without an external appearance.

Or internal substance.
Only people like this are capable of entering the Water Heaven.
However I did meet a saint in the Water Heaven. He was a Patriarch of Zen Buddhism- Bodhidharma.

***

We know that:
The Patriarch Bodhidharma hailed from the people of Dili of Southern Tianzhu, and was the third son of the Emperor Xiangzhi.
He later met Prajnatara, the twenty-seventh Zen Patriarch, and became the twenty-eighth Patriarch Bodhidharma.
In the first year of Putong of the Liang Dynasty, Patriarch Bodhidharma sailed by sea to Guangzhou. The emperor welcomed him and took him to Jianye (the capital).
The emperor questioned him: "Since becoming emperor, I have built temples and written sutras. What merit do I have?"
Patriarch Bodhidharma answered: "No merit."
He then asked: "What is true merit?"
The response was: "Purified wisdom is wondrous and flawless. Essence originated from non-material and tranquil formlessness; such merit cannot be obtained from the material world."
He questioned again: "What is the absolute noble truth?"
Patriarch Bodhidharma answered: "There is no such nobility in this wide universe."
He questioned: "Who is it facing the emperor?"
Patriarch Bodhidharma answered: "I don't know him."
The emperor did not understand.
Afterwards the Patriarch Bodhidharma crossed the local river and retreated for nine years at the Shaolin Temple at Mt. Song. Eventually he passed his teaching on to Huike and the verse of his dharma passing was:

I being here,
Teach dharma to save sentient beings,
One flower will grow five petals,
Its fruit will be accomplished naturally.

***

The Patriarch Bodhidharma sang a verse when he saw that I had arrived at the Water Heaven:

There is a desire to be pure but is it ever.
One can talk about the void yet not necessarily emptiness.
Pitiful Lu Sheng-yen.
Half the body is in the morass.

As soon as I turned my head and saw that it was Patriarch Bodhidharma, I replied with my own verse:

A great patriarch of the people.
Does not know Lu Sheng-yen.
Teaches Zen yet not necessarily Zen.
How could there be a meeting in half a body.

The Patriarch Bodhidharma laughed out loud and said, "What a clever-toothed sharp mouth is Lu Sheng-yen! Since you are in the Water Heaven it will be good for me to corroborate with you."

Here is a poem:

Debate Zen in the Water Heaven.
The heavenly realm has an afterglow.
Both give astonishing words.
Passed down to the world and become awakening tallies.

23. What do Sutras Explain?

In the Water Heaven I met the Patriarch Bodhidharma during my sixth round of deep meditation. Subsequently a debate began.

The Patriarch Bodhidharma asked, "What is wide, in the middle, and a summary?"

I answered, "Small, medium, and large."

The Patriarch Bodhidharma responded with another question, "What is a summary?"

I answered, "It explains a commentary."

The Patriarch Bodhidharma asked, "But what is a commentary?"

I responded, "It explains sutra."

The Patriarch Bodhidharma asked, "But what is a sutra? What does it explain?"(Absolute truth.)

I answered, "A sutra records what the Buddha said. It also explains that the Buddha simply did not give any dharma talks."

The Patriarch Bodhidharma opened his copper-colored bell-shaped eyes widely and gave a loud shout, "Whoa! A question that from the beginning could not be answered is now answered by Grand Master Lu. You are truly not someone to be taken lightly; no wonder you are so radiant! Grand Master Lu, throughout the whole world, there is no one, other than you, with your superlative wisdom.

In return, I asked the Patriarch Bodhidharma, "Among Bodhisattvas, supreme wisdom belongs to Manjusri Bodhisattva. Among Arhats, supreme wisdom is mastered by Sariputra. And in this world, supreme wisdom is mastered by Grand Master Lu. Then may I ask Patriarch Bodhidharma, what realm are you in? What rank is your wisdom?"

The Patriarch Bodhidharma laughed out loud, "Do you know Dharma?"(The Absolute Truth subtle jab.)

I answered, "I do not know." (The Absolute Truth response.)

The Patriarch Bodhidharma asked me back, "You do not know Grand Master Lu, what realm I am in? Or the height of my wisdom?"

This question which I originally asked was now asked back by the Patriarch Bodhidharma. If I replied incorrectly, the Patriarch would laugh at me. If I answered with nothing but clever evasions, I would still lose one point. My reply needed to be right on target. Just then, I recalled the response the Patriarch Bodhidharma had given to Emperor Liang. And it happened to be the right timing to reply with in return.

I answered, "Broad without boundaries, originating from the void and tranquil, how can there be a first."

The Patriarch Bodhidharma listened and nodded.

I then asked him, "Why did you leave only one straw sandal after you passed away? Why not both straw sandals?"

The Patriarch Bodhidharma answered, "Seeking a soul mate."

"Isn't Shenquang (Huike) the soul mate?"

He answered, "Huike is one shoe. The other shoe is Grand Master Lu."

I asked, "Why me?"

He responded, "Because only you asked. No one else did!"

Poem:

Truly a sage.
Changing to the Water Heaven form.
Spirit exists distinctly.
Who can distinguish true from false.

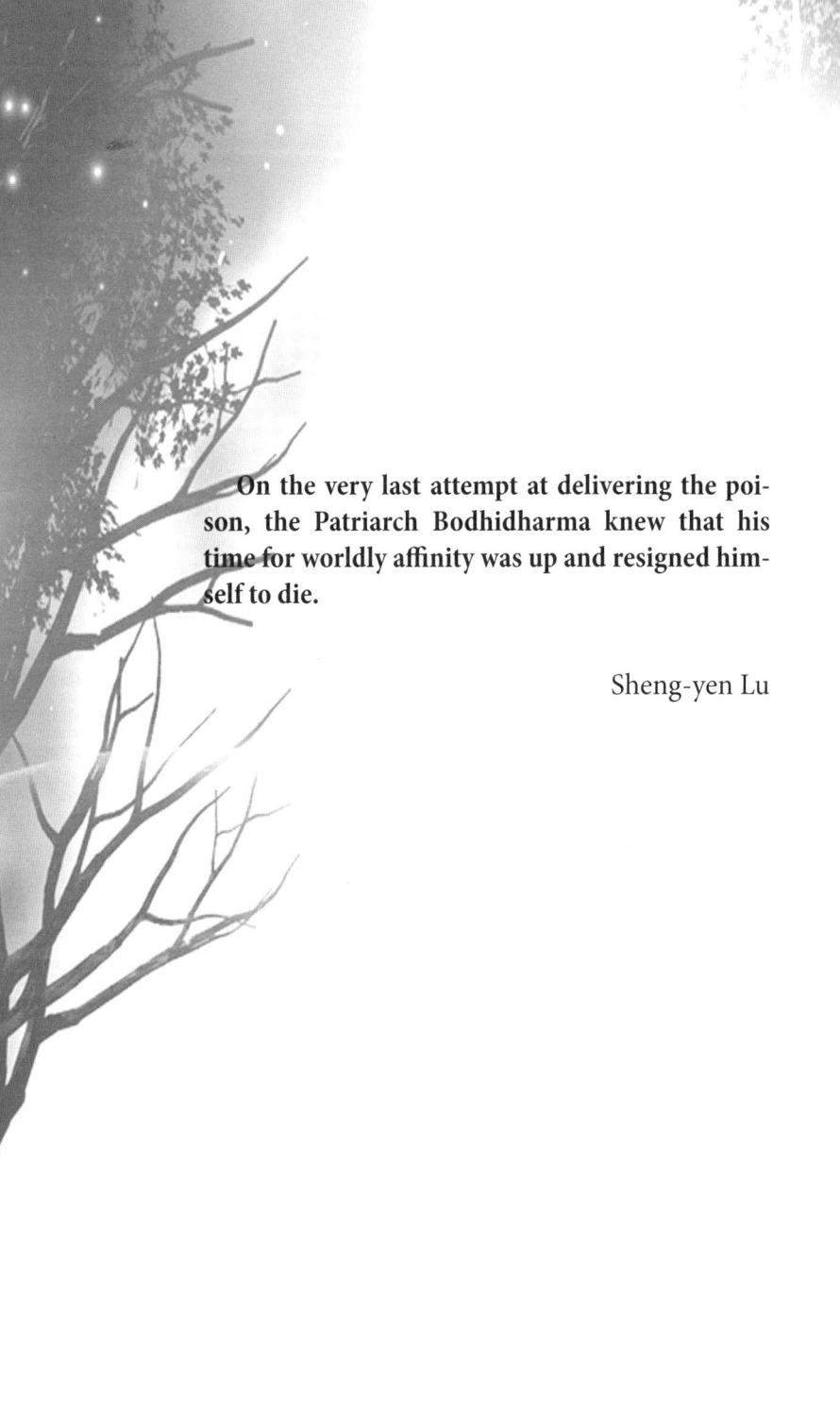

On the very last attempt at delivering the poison, the Patriarch Bodhidharma knew that his time for worldly affinity was up and resigned himself to die.

Sheng-yen Lu

24. Bodhiruci

In the Water Heaven I met up with the Patriarch Bodhidharma. We began to chat about Bodhiruci's past.

Bodhiruci was an Indian, who knew the Tripitaka, Sutras, Abhidharma, and Vinaya very thoroughly. He arrived in China before the Patriarch Bodhidharma, and became a national teacher.

After the Patriarch Bodhidharma arrived in China, Bodhiruci competed with the Patriarch Bodhidharma over their Buddhist teaching. Bodhiruci could not compete and became afraid that his position as a national teacher would not last. He therefore decided to hinder the Patriarch Bodhidharma's efforts to save sentient beings wherever possible.

Bodhiruci was proficient in Buddhist Dharma. His supernatural powers were superlative and he could easily command:

    Asuras,
    Yaksas,
    Dragons,
    Ju Mo Luo,
    Laksmi, and
    Apsara deities.

Bodhiruci spread a rumour that the Patriarch Bodhidharma had had an affair with an Apsara deity.

He also said that the Buddhist teachings of the Patriarch Bodhidharma were not true Buddhism but a cult-masked "evil religion."

He said that the Patriarch Bodhidharma desired only fame, fortune, and power and was a pursuer of authority.

He also said that the Patriarch Bodhidharma knew only evil practices; he did not have true lineage; and his superlative wisdom was false.

Furthermore he said that those who followed the Patriarch Bodhidharma were the descendents of evil. They would suffer misfortunes while living and descend to hell after death.

...

In order to strengthen his position as the national teacher, Bodhiruci ordered someone to deliver a toxicant for the Patriarch Bodhidharma to take.

For the first four or five attempts, they were unsuccessful.

On the very last attempt at delivering the poison, the Patriarch Bodhidharma knew that his time for worldly affinity was up and resigned himself to die.

***

I asked, "Why did Bodhiruci, who had great knowledge about Buddhist dharma, and excellent supernatural powers, have such strong worldly desires?"

The Patriarch Bodhidharma answered, "Had leaks."

I asked, "How did Bodhiruci's life end up finally?"

Patriarch Bodhidharma replied, "Where is the lasting enlightenment?"

I asked, "Why did Bodhiruci, who understood the Tripitaka, go to the other side?"

The Patriarch Bodhidharma answered, "Although he understood the Tripitaka, he is not out of the Tripitaka."

I asked, "Bodhiruci framed you so many times, does the Patriarch have any special thoughts about this?"

The Patriarch Bodhidharma responded, "I am thankful for the offerings."

I asked, "Bodhiruci possessed all six supernatural powers, why then did he ride a fake boat?"

The Patriarch Bodhidharma answered, "Having six supernatural powers is not having six supernatural powers."

The Patriarch Bodhidharma said to me, "You, Grand Master Lu, as expected, act very anxious like a mother towards her child!"

Poem:

A true one will not be materialistic.
Buddha and evil compete.
Bodhiruci,
Contemporary rosy-colored clouds at dawn.
(This and previous writings contain the absolute truth; they are possibly difficult to understand.)

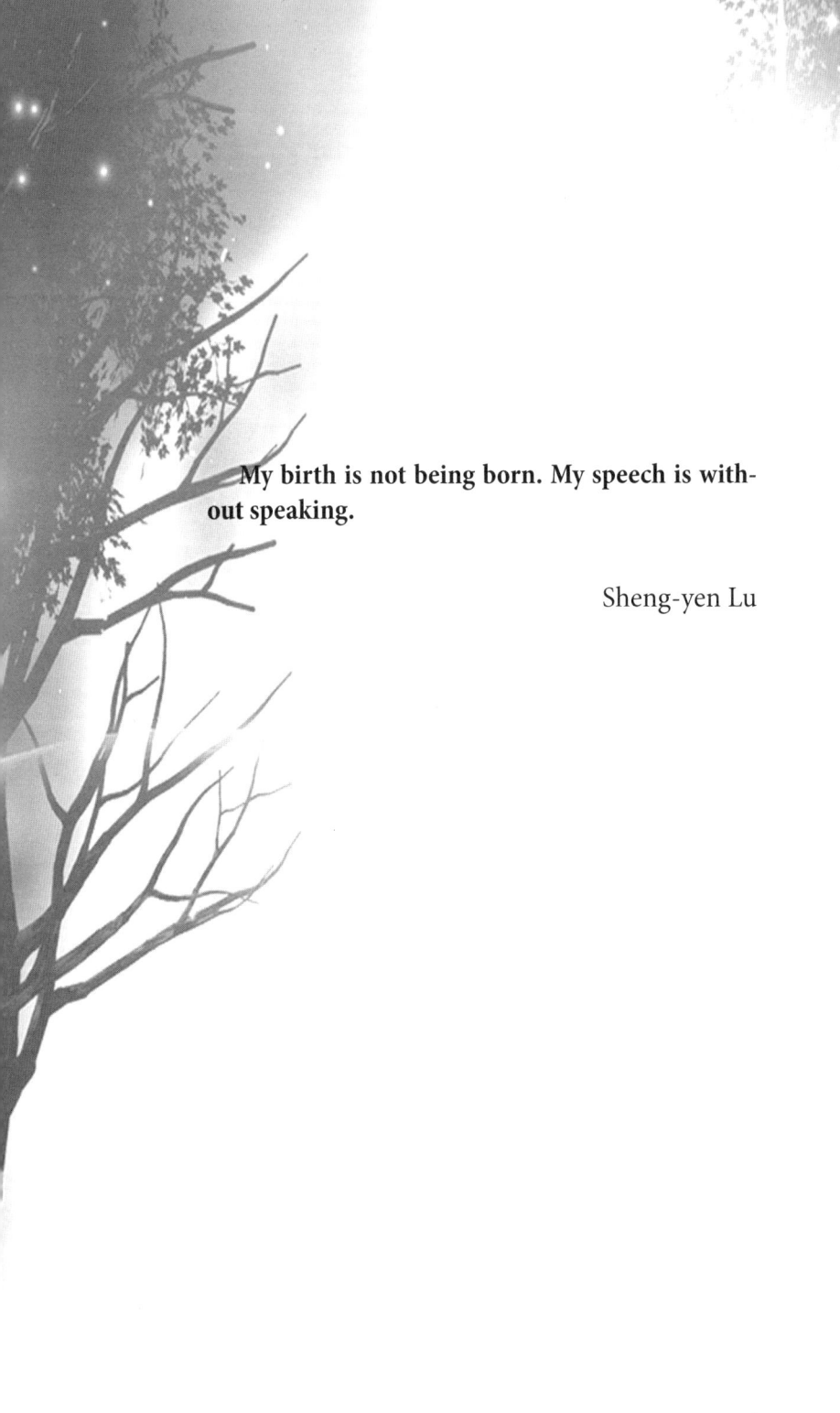

My birth is not being born. My speech is without speaking.

Sheng-yen Lu

25. The Buddha, Bodhidharma, and Grand Master Lu

In the Water Heaven, the Patriarch Bodhidharma and I had a formal face-to-face dialogue.

The Patriarch Bodhidharma questioned, "Grand Master Lu, fish in the water must have water to live, but why do they also die in the water?"

I answered, "In the saha world I need air to survive, yet all the same I will die in the air."

The Patriarch Bodhidharma said, "That is so, that is so."

I said, "Heavens, heavens."

The Patriarch Bodhidharma then asked, "Did Grand Master Lu see the Buddha?"

I replied, "The Buddha's body is filled with the Dharma realm, of course I can see him any time any place."

The Patriarch Bodhidharma questioned, "What did the Buddha tell you?"

I answered, "I know you."

The Patriarch Bodhidharma questioned further, "Know you what?"

I did not answer with any words. Instead, I showed him the posture of the "Golden Rooster Standing on One Leg," with the left hand holding a lotus flower and the right hand in the Dharma-speaking mudra.

I then added, "My birth is not being born. My speech is without speaking."

The Patriarch Bodhidharma was stunned, "Grand Master Lu, I confirmed today that you indeed possess the Dharma treasure of righteous eyes and wondrous mind of nirvana. Shakyamuni Buddha's enlightenment and yours are identical and no different."

The Patriarch Bodhidharma added, "This is the utmost wisdom of the Buddha. Today, you Grand Master Lu have gained the same utmost wisdom. Buddha, Bodhidharma, and Grand Master Lu are totally one and the same. This is the highest wisdom. There is no wisdom higher."

The Patriarch Bodhidharma went on, "You have Maitreya Bodhisattva's *The Divine Book* in your heart. Why don't you take a look at what is written there?"

I consulted the book inwardly.

A sentence was written, "Buddha was never born."

On seeing it, I was greatly delighted and understood clearly without any ifs or buts.

The Patriarch Bodhidharma said, "In the current era, your wisdom is already in first place. No one can compete. You are today's first patriarch. Because of your existence in this world all sages will enter nirvana, not to mention those living Buddhas, masters, and those with stature.

I replied, "It is just a temporary evolutionary process."

The Patriarch Bodhidharma said, "Once this utmost wisdom has been gained, it is gained forever."

I answered, "I do not dare."

The Patriarch Bodhidharma responded, "Our encounter is illusion seeing illusion. The Water Heaven is the affinity. My confirmation is an illusion. You must also know too that your existence is an illusion!"

Poem:

Encounters have no time and space.
Enlightenment is without east or west.
Everything turns out to be an illusion.
Bitterness and happiness are all just dreams.

As long as one is able to find the right medicine any disease will be cured.

Sheng-yen Lu

26. A Cure for Chronic Ringworm

Yingru, a newly wed, gave birth to a baby that had spots all over its body. Its head, face, four limbs, and torso were all covered with blotches of chronic ringworm fungus.

She brought the little baby to see me.

I looked at it and was taken aback.

I drew a "skin-treating talisman" for the baby to drink with the water treated with it.

But it was not effective.

I then blessed the baby with the Vajra Finger but this too resulted in little improvement.

I was out of options. Suddenly, I remembered *The Divine Book*.

I consulted *The Divine Book* and found the passage:

"Immediately find King Jia Luoluo!"

Therefore, while in meditation, my illusory body traveled to the Firmament City of the universe.

The Firmament City has three kings:

1. King Jia Luoluo
2. King Garuda

3. King Jialing Pinjia

***

It turned out that of these three kings of the Firmament City: Jia Luoluo is king of the nine-phoenixes; Garuda, is king of the birds; and Jialing Pinjia, king of exquisite-song birds. Firmament City is the kingdom of bird country.

Jialuoluo asked me, "What brought you here?"

I replied, "A baby in the saha world has chronic ringworm all over leaving no clear skin visible. I am at loss not knowing how to cure it?"

Jialuoluo answered, "You came to the right place! The saliva of my nine-phoenixes happens to be the nemesis for all types of ringworm. In fact it can cure any skin disease. Take it back and apply it to the talismans that you drew and the baby will be cured."

I was very happy to hear this.

I thanked King Jialuoluo.

King Jialuoluo responded, "The great name Grand Master Lu, we all have known well. We also know that you have realized the enlightenment of Buddha. Call me anytime whenever you need me in the future and I will come to assist you."

I took the "nine-phoenix saliva" and as soon as my illusory body departed from Firmament City, I carried out the treatment.

Yingru's little baby is getting better.

Luwen has convalesced.

Luoquan is completely clean!

***

I came to profoundly realize that, from the beginning there has been a phenomenon whereby there is always a way for one to conquer another. The same truth applies to illness. As long as one is able to find the right medicine any disease will be cured.

Maitreya Bodhisattva gave me *The Divine Book*. By simply browsing through *The Divine Book*, the answers are revealed. It turns out that when it comes to skin diseases, King Jialuoluo is the one to find. The chronic ringworm was at first an illness that was extremely difficult to cure. However, under my treatment, the baby's ringworm infections were all cured. My reputation has now spread throughout the country, to the north and south, and in all ten directions. I am now busier than ever.

Poem:

> *Desire healthy skin.*
> *Must seek the King of Nine-Phoenixes.*
> *Fly to the Firmament City.*
> *A cure is hopeful.*

Cancer in students who strongly believed in me disappeared and this greatly surprised their doctors.

Sheng-yen Lu

27. Cancer "Breaker"

I was so astonished when I realized that many people around me had developed cancer and died from it; one person here, another there, many of my friends, and many of my classmates.

Cancer, cancer, cancer, cancer, cancer, ...

"Why are there so many cancer cases?" (Simply too many people get cancer.)

One day, a student from Romania came and told me that she had cancer. Her name was Meehila.

There were many cancerous lesions on her neck.

I was very anxious.

So I decided to to consult *The Divine Book*. In it, was written, "Go to the city of Shanjian in the Heaven of Indra and find celestial doctor Gipoduo."

My illusory body went to the city of Shanjian and found celestial doctor Gipoduo.

Gipoduo told me that:

"Cancers" are aged cells.

"Cancers" are mutant cells.

"Cancers" are pathologically changed cells.

"Cancers" are dead cells.
"Cancers" are poisoned cells.
"Cancers" are infected cells.

I questioned the celestial doctor, "How should one treat it?"

The celestial doctor replied, "In the human realm, there are only two ways. One way is to remove the cancer. The other is to use chemotherapy."

I said, "This I know."

I asked, "What if it is me?"

The celestial doctor laughed loudly and said, "Grand Master Lu you have accomplished an illusory body. You also possess a mystical illusory hand. It can enter a human body and remove cancer cells just like it is picking grapes! The cancer patient will then be cured."

I said, "I only need to use the illusory hand?"

The celestial doctor answered, "Yes, this is correct, just use the illusory hand."

I asked, "Does this method require any preconditions?"

The celestial doctor replied, "Those who believe in you, pray to you, and chant your heart mantra will receive a response. With the illusory hand, you can remove their cancer cells. Cancer cancer cancer cancer cancer will all be plucked by your illusory hand! They will suddenly disappear."

The celestial doctor continued, "These disciples will see you in their dreams. They will see your illusory hands entering their body and removing all the bad cells."

Ah! I finally understood!

Therefore, I was eventually able to utilize the illusory body, the body outside my physical body, to save cancer patients everywhere. Cancer in students who strongly believed in me disappeared and this greatly surprised their doctors.

The female student from Romania was cured of cancer.

Many cancer students went into remission.

Poem:

Life-death separation in the human realm.
People with cancer are in agony.
Only pray to Grand Master Lu,
The illusory hand cures the disease.

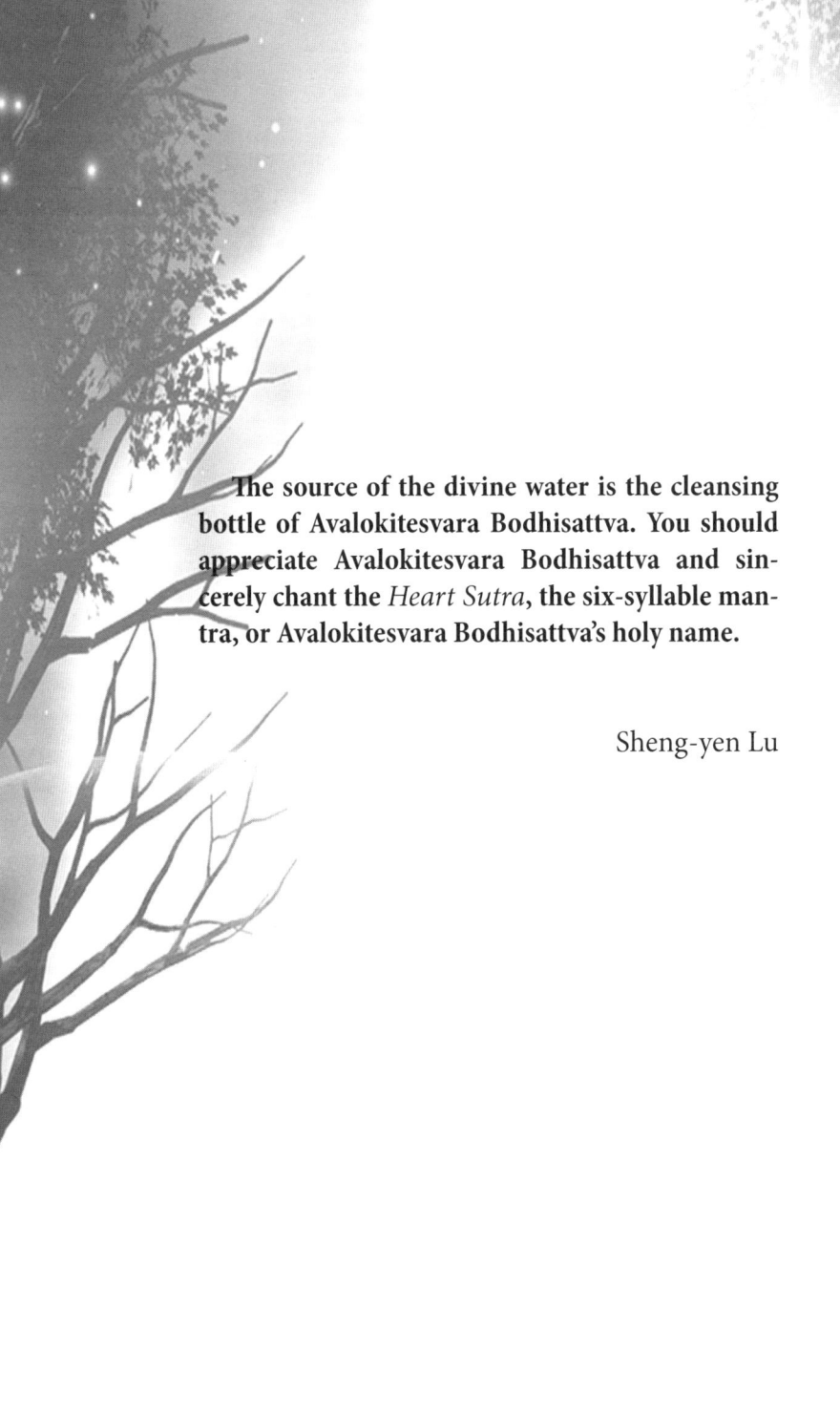

The source of the divine water is the cleansing bottle of Avalokitesvara Bodhisattva. You should appreciate Avalokitesvara Bodhisattva and sincerely chant the *Heart Sutra*, the six-syllable mantra, or Avalokitesvara Bodhisattva's holy name.

Sheng-yen Lu

28. True "Brainwashing"

The child Yangyi was born with a flat affect, just like a person with an intellectual disability.

Although he was already six years old his speech was slurred. He was incapable of learning anything from his parents.

Externally, he looked normal, but in fact, he was retarded. He forgot everything.

He could not count from one to hundred.

He was unable to add, subtract, multiply, or divide.

He needed help with eating, dressing, living, and transportation; such as putting his clothes on and feeding himself.

Already six years old, he still did not know how to use the rest room; he would wet or soil his pants.

His parents were very anxious so they brought him to see me. I opened *The Divine Book* to consult. It turned out that the passage that appeared had two characters "brain-washing."

***

I exited in my illusory body. Then I entered one of Yangyi's dreams.

In the dream he saw Grand Master Lu take him to the Heavenly River.

There I opened his head. I then washed it thoroughly with the Heavenly River water. Many filthy objects were washed off. Many knots in the brain were also untied.

Finally I closed his head and stitched it back together.

Thereafter, Grand Master Lu returned Yangyi from the "Heavenly River" back to his dream. He was in the dream the whole time.

Strange things then began to happen.

From the moment Yangyi had the dream, all his memories were restored completely. His speech became clear. He was able to take care of everything himself. Eating, clothing, living, and moving, all became normal.

He could remember things assigned to him.

No one needed to show him how to use restroom.

He learned his school work quickly.

Six-year old Yangyi now became a "gifted child."

After reading a book once, he was able to remember everything.

The concerns that the parents of Yangyi originally had for their slow-witted child were now all swept away. He had become superior compared to normal children.

I told the parents of Yangyi, "The child was cured because his brain was cleaned by the divine water of the Heavenly River. The source of the divine water is the cleansing bottle of Avalokitesvara Bodhisattva. You should appreciate Avalokitesvara Bodhisattva and sincerely chant the *Heart Sutra*, the six-syllable mantra, or Avalokitesvara Bodhisattva's holy name.

The parents of Yangyi carried out the chant practices.

Word spread throughout Taiwan and I became known as the divine doctor.

Once a monk had the same problem, forgetting immediately what he just read, unable to remember anything at all.

He dreamed about the arrival of Grand Master Lu, and being taken to Heavenly River for a "brainwashing."

On waking up from the dream, at each glance he was able to read ten lines at a time and completely memorize them. He was able to remember an entire sutra.

The monk made a special trip over to thank me for such a majestic incidence.

The human world has "brainwashing."

Heaven also has Heavenly River "brainwashing."

When hearing these true stories, one cannot help but be respectful of Grand Master Lu's "Heavenly River brainwashing."

Poem:

> *Able to wash one's brain in the Heavenly River.*
> *It is a shocking fact in the human world.*
> *But the incident is true.*
> *Brightness enters the palace steps.*

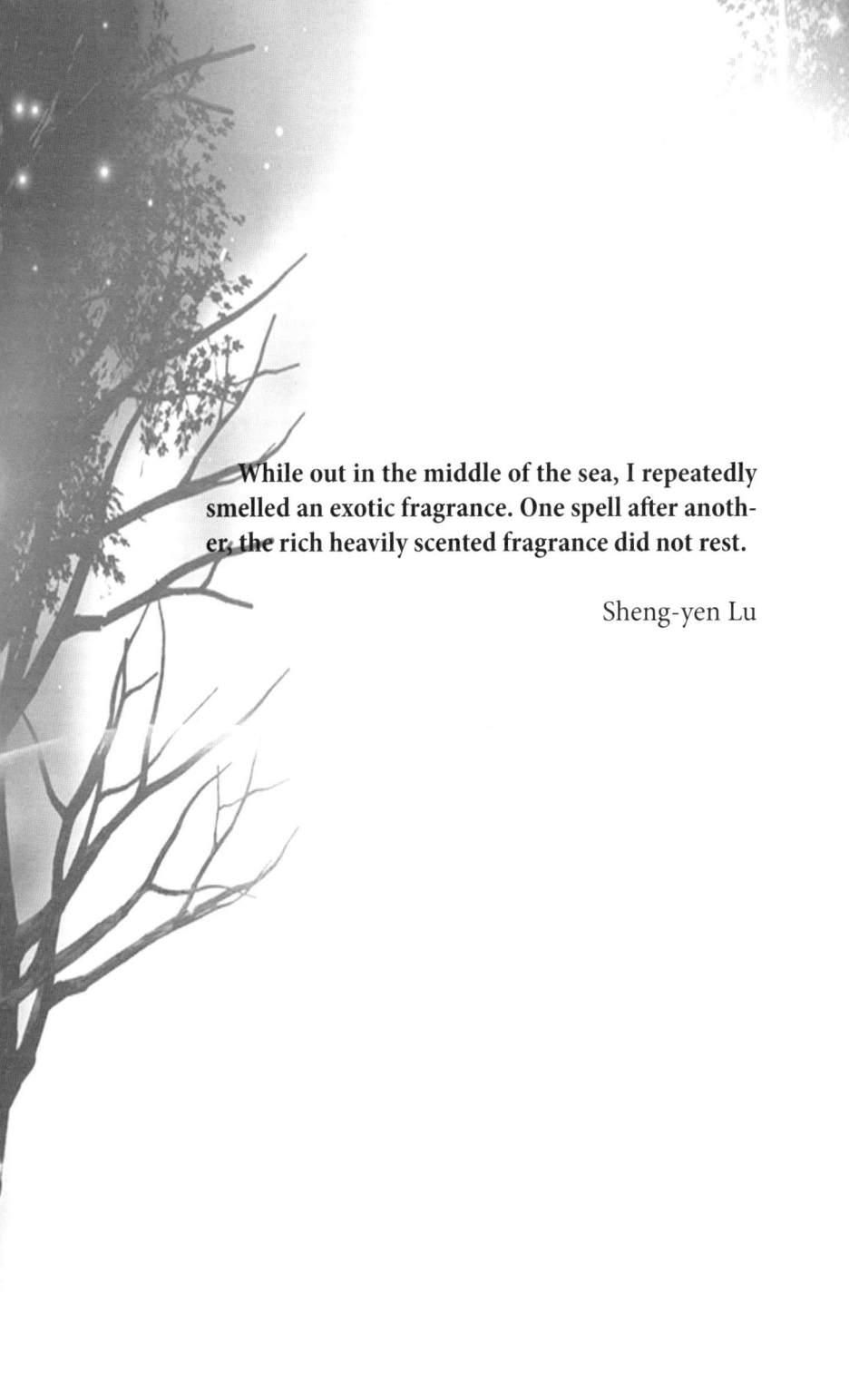

While out in the middle of the sea, I repeatedly smelled an exotic fragrance. One spell after another, the rich heavily scented fragrance did not rest.

Sheng-yen Lu

29. Hurry Off, Dragon King

I was at the seashore on Kemaite Island. The ocean was calm without waves. All of a sudden, the wind picked up and the sea became rough.

It turned out that the Eight Great Dragon Kings had come to take refuge with me.

The scene at the time was witnessed by Master Lianxin along with others. It was indeed mind-blowing.

It was a sunny day.

The wind had subsided.

The sea was peaceful.

Then suddenly the sea surged up into eight separate stormy waves.

Master Lianti also said, "Even the Eight Great Dragon Kings came to take refuge. It was truly inconceivable!"

***

Another time I was out taking a boat out to sea. That day was also sunny and there was no wind. The boat was moving extremely steadily. The sky was blue. The ocean was blue. It looked just like a great

landscape painting.
I remembered a poem:

Daily blue sky.
Blue sky daily.

And:

Small country land.
Gentle kasaya robes.
Bright waves ocean surface.
A full circle jade sky.

Such a pleasant poem, such a pleasant day, such a pleasant sea, and such a pleasant cruise completely relaxed everybody. Everyone was very joyful.

While out in the middle of the sea, I repeatedly smelled an exotic fragrance. One spell after another, the rich heavily scented fragrance did not rest.

Suddenly -

Stormy waves started to break.

The waves became turbulent.

The roaring wind and surging waves tossed our boat like a leaf in a whirlwind.

The wind blew stronger and stronger. The waves reached higher and higher. The small boat almost tipped over.

A few students threw up.

Some held tightly to the mast or a chair.

Some chanted mantras.

The wind behaved strangely. The waves also were mysteriously huge. How was it that at one moment the wind and waves were calm and peaceful, then in the blink of an eye, the boat would inevitably sink?

One student yelled, "Look, a great black wave!"

Another one yelled, "Grand Master Lu save us!"

I focused internally and consulted *The Divine Book*. The passage it revealed was, "The Dragon King comes to see Grand Master Lu."

Suddenly I realized that the fragrance I smelled was the "Scent of the Dragon's Saliva." The large wave had been caused by the Dragon King and the arrival of his entourage. They had all come to have audience with me, the Dharma King (The King of Buddha Kings.)

I stood on the bow of the boat

In the void, I wrote four characters: "Dragon King leave immediately!"

As soon as I had finished writing the four characters, the wind stopped, the waves calmed down, and the surface of the sea was restored to complete tranquillity. It made what had just occurred seem simply like a dream. It was inconceivably difficult to imagine.

Poem:

> *The wind blows so the waves fly.*
> *The clouds obstructs the rays of the sun.*
> *It is the Dragon King's arrival to have an audience.*
> *For safety quickly order him to leave!*

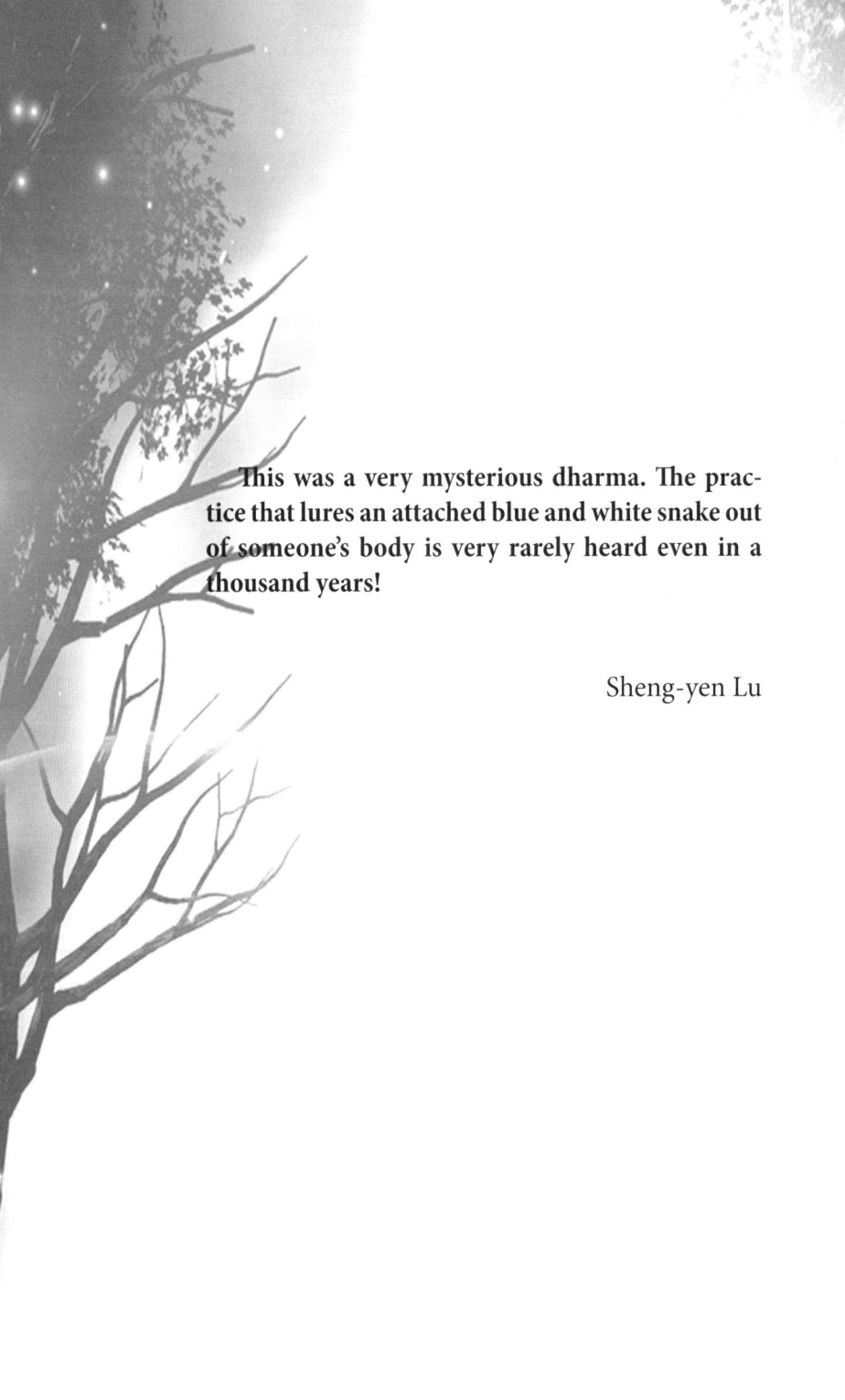

This was a very mysterious dharma. The practice that lures an attached blue and white snake out of someone's body is very rarely heard even in a thousand years!

Sheng-yen Lu

30. The Snake and Mouse

One of my disciples Shan Xiao became ill with an unusual and painful illness. Why was the illness considered strange?

It was because his pain moved around.

One moment it was the head that was hurting. The next moment, the pain was at the soles of his feet. It then moved to the throat, his four limbs, his heart, stomach, back, front of his chest, and finally his shoulders and waist.

Shan Xiao's pain was so severe that he cried out for his father and screamed for his mother!

He certainly consulted with all the specialists.

But no causes could be identified.

No injection had any effect.

Any medicine he took was in vain.

Acupuncture did not help.

Massages cured nothing.

Even complete body scans could not diagnose what was causing his aches and pains.

Eventually he came to see me.

Using my divine eye I carefully looked all over him. I immediately saw one long thin blue and white snake crawling inside throughout Shan Xiao's whole body. His pain followed wherever the snake was.

What could be done to help him?

I turned my thoughts inward and consulted *The Divine Book* and it revealed one Chinese character, "Mouse."

But at that moment I was confused.

What did it mean by "mouse"?

I was pondering over the "mouse" character and wondering what could be the association between the blue and white snake and a mouse.

A short time later, one day while in meditation I saw Mahamayuri Vidyaraja.

Mahamayuri Vidyaraja said to me, "Grand Master Lu, Shan Xiao's pain is caused by the blue and white snake. The best way to lure the blue and white snake out of Shan Xiao is to use a mouse as bait. Shan Xiao must chant your heart mantra. Grand Master Lu must perform the boundary protection dharma as soon as the snake leaps out of his body; only then can his pain be cured!"

***

I had seen the one "mouse" Chinese character in *The Divine Book*. Additionally, I received inspiration from Mahamayuri Vidyaraja. At last I understood.

I first asked the layman Shan Xiao to chant the Root Guru's Heart mantra during meditation, *Om, gu-ru, lian-sheng, sid-dhi, hum*.

Then right in front of Shan Xiao, I placed a mouse inside an iron cage.

In this way, approximately half an hour passed.

When Shan Xiao merely hiccuped, as soon as his mouth opened, the blue and white snake flew out, went straight to the "mouse" and bit it while the mouse was still in the iron cage.

The mouse squeaked horribly and died.

The blue and white snake attempted to return to Shan Xiao's body. But by this time I had already done the boundary protection dharma on Shan Xiao's body.

The blue and white snake had no choice; it could only stick out it's tongue, wag it's tail, and depart! (Invisible.)

Since this practice was performed, Shan Xiao's pain has healed completely.

This was a very mysterious dharma. The practice that lures an attached blue and white snake out of someone's body is very rarely heard even in a thousand years!

The matter became quite a legend.

Every one talked about it with interest!

Poem:

What resides inside the body.
The pain makes one miserable.
Yet only prayers and "The Divine Book" can come to the rescue.
The snake spirit then rushes away.

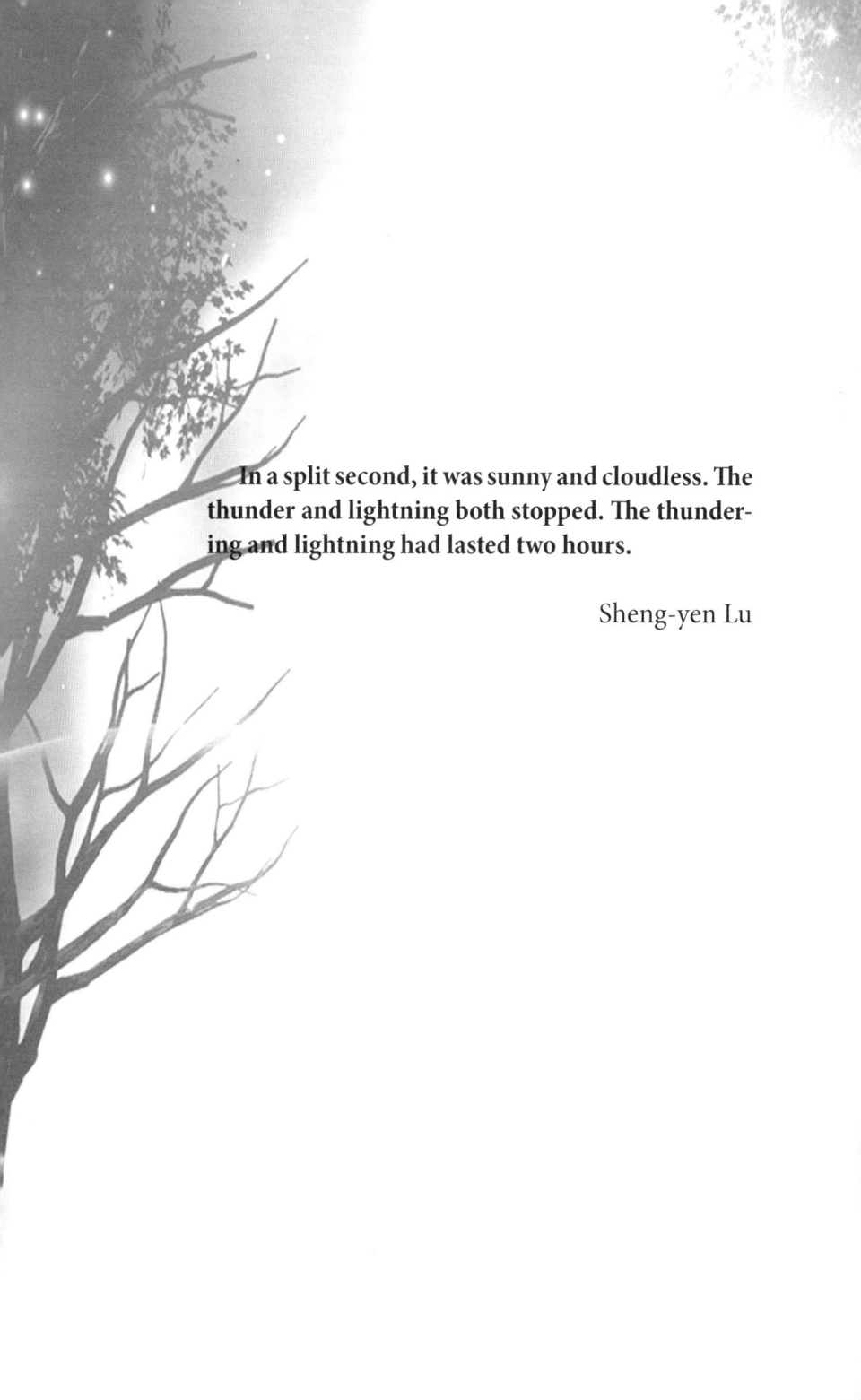

In a split second, it was sunny and cloudless. The thunder and lightning both stopped. The thundering and lightning had lasted two hours.

Sheng-yen Lu

31. A Thunder Rumbling Day

On the morning of July 1, 2008, I had just sat down quietly to start my practice, when the sound of thunder began rumbling one after another. Lightning struck across the sky flash after flash. The thunder and lightning were continuous.

This reminded me of a little town in China where they experienced frequent thunder and lightning.

One time, the thunder and lightning occurred non-stop more than four thousand times.

It was said that:
    Many houses were burned.
    Countless trees were struck.
    Seven people were hit by lightning and died.

Days with thundering like this are rare and hardly seen in Seattle in the United States.

Lightning came down from all directions.

The rumble of thunder shook the heavens. It made a tearing sound and moved the earth.

"Pi Li Pa La"

The earth jumped from the shaking and rumbling. Sand was flying and rocks were leaping. The sky was covered and the sun became invisible. One bolt of lightning, followed another moment of thunder; sometimes eight flashes of lightning all occurred together. The rumbling sound made people deaf.

I wondered, "What is happening?"

The lightning surrounded my house like electric snakes, crashing down continuously.

The rumbling sound of thunder was happening right above the roof causing the floor to "mambo."

I raised a question to the void, "Why are you shooting at me?"

From the void, Ninth-Heaven-In-Yuan-Thunderclap-Puhua Deity answered me, "I am catching the escaped Eight-Claw Demon."

I questioned, "But how can the Eight-Claw Demon be here?"

Ninth-Heaven-In-Yuan-Thunderclap-Puhua Deity replied, "I saw the demon hiding inside your house. However all of sudden it disappeared. It is very strange?"

I did not say any more and continued my practice. While practicing, my crown released three lights: Buddha light, Bright light, and Divine light.

Once the three lights were released, the Thunder Father, Lightning Mother, and Thunder Division deity left in a hurry.

In a split second, it was sunny and cloudless. The thunder and lightning both stopped. The thundering and lightning had lasted two hours. Everything returned to normal after the two hours.

I stood up in front of the shrine.

An eight-foot golden beetle fell off my kasaya. The golden beetle seemingly paid homage to me three times. It crawled and crawled, then flew out through a window and disappeared.

I was very surprised. How could an eight-foot golden beetle be on my kasaya.

I looked inside and consulted *The Divine Book*. It stated: "Mistakenly saved a demon!"

Ah! The golden beetle was the Eight-Claw Demon.

I again looked within and consulted *The Divine Book*. What should one do?

The book revealed two Chinese characters that meant "affinity."

Poem:

> *Eight-Claw demon flies.*
> *Thunder and lightning chase it fiercely.*
> *Words for the demon,*
> *"Sincerely repent!"*

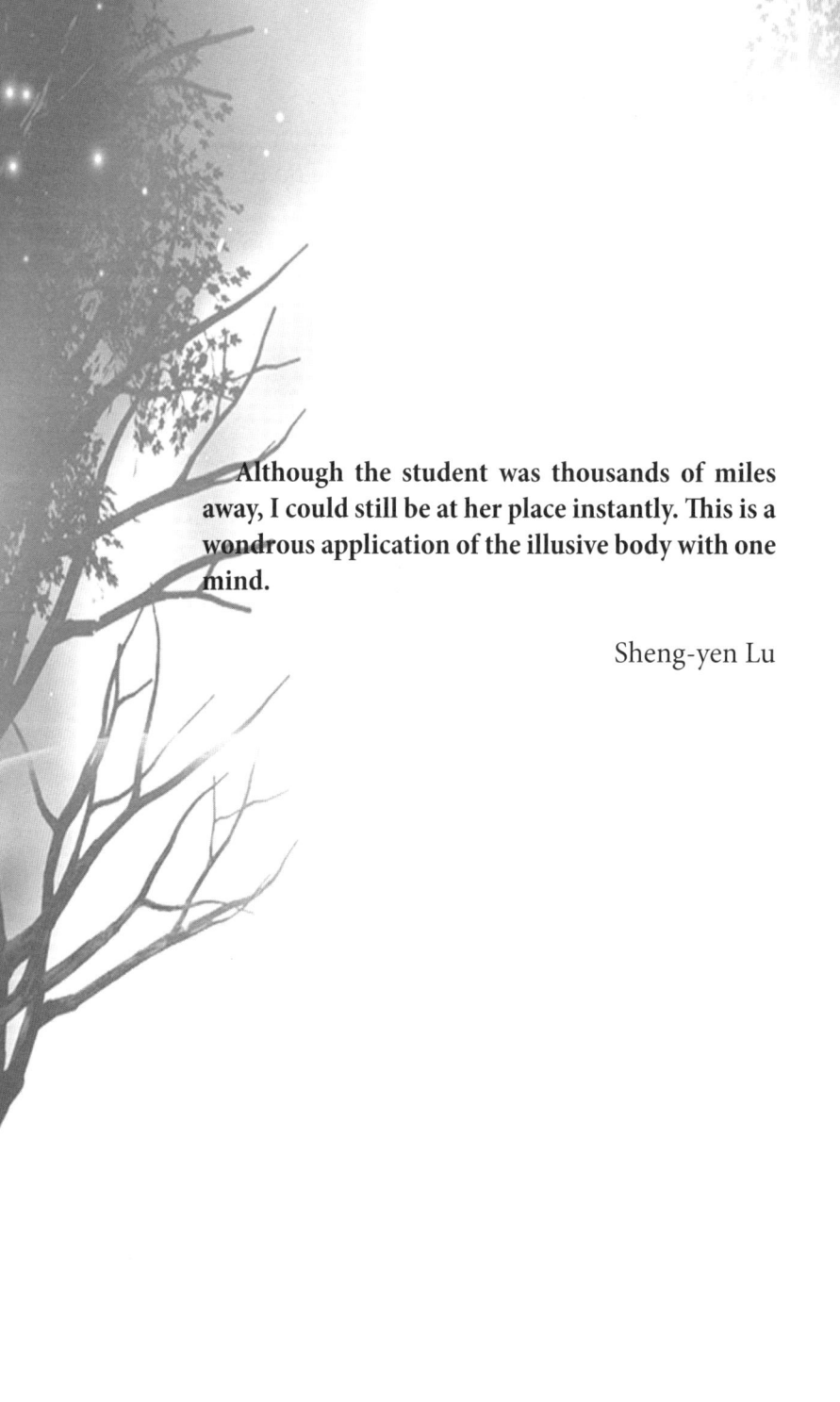

Although the student was thousands of miles away, I could still be at her place instantly. This is a wondrous application of the illusive body with one mind.

Sheng-yen Lu

32. A Sudden "Impulse"

On the night of July 6, 2008, Master Lianxiang, Xiaofeng Chen, and I were in a supermarket.

The main purpose was for Master Lianxiang to shop for a special kind of soap. The special soap needed to be:

Natural.

No added fragrance.

Not strangely fabricated.

Not irritating.

Only this kind of soap can be used by those with a sensitive constitution, so it will not cause an allergic reaction.

The three of us were walking in the supermarket.

Suddenly, a blow of intangible force materialized above my head and shook my heart.

This was a sudden "impulse" which is hard to describe.

My entire body froze.

Qi moved from my feet to my head and reached my "Baihui Acupoint"

All my skin's pores opened up wide and emitted brightness.

All of sudden a fragrant scent pervaded everywhere.

Qi moved inside my body and touched my heart.

I said to Master Lianxiang and Xiaofeng Chen, "I need to concentrate for a moment, and closed my eyes a while."

I moved to the side, to a quiet place. I stood still and innerly observed *The Divine Book*. It stated: "Huilin will soon die."

I immediately kept myself standing with one hand holding onto a food counter. My illusory body instantly flew out and arrived in front of the one who was about to die.

***

About this laywoman Huilin.

While group disciples were chanting "Grand Master's Heart Mantra," it was seen that Grand Master Lian-sheng arrived and transformed to Amitabha. Avalokiteshvara was on his right, and Mahasthamaprapta, left. The three Western Saints came to receive laywoman Huilin.

Laywoman Huilin was saying: "Grand Master Lu transformed to Buddha in the middle with Avalokiteshvara on the right side and Mahasthamaprapta on the left. The Western Pure Land appears on the top. We will be going to west together after my ninth level lotus appears."

As soon as she finished speaking, laywoman Huilin passed away.

(It was discovered that the laywoman Huilin knew that her time was almost up. She wrote a letter to True Buddha Quarter. In the letter, she requested that Grand Master Lu deliver her. I promised her that I would deliver her in person.)

***

Laywoman Huilin had yelled loudly when she was passing away: "Grand Master Lu delivers me."

She screamed loudly: "*Om, gu-ru, lian-sheng, sid-dhi, hum!*"

That was why I got the sudden "impulse" in the supermarket. Even though it happened in a supermarket, I was still able to hold on to a food counter with one hand, stand still, exit in the illusory body, and deliver the disciple. Although the student was thousands of miles away, I could still be at her place instantly. This is a wondrous application of the illusive body with one mind.

Master Lianxiang and Xiaofeng Chen asked, "What happened?"

I replied, "I had to take care of something."

Poem:

Avalokiteshvara assists in remote delivery.
Mahasthamaprapta compliments remote reception.
Grand Master Lu appears above.
Great brightness of the pure land.

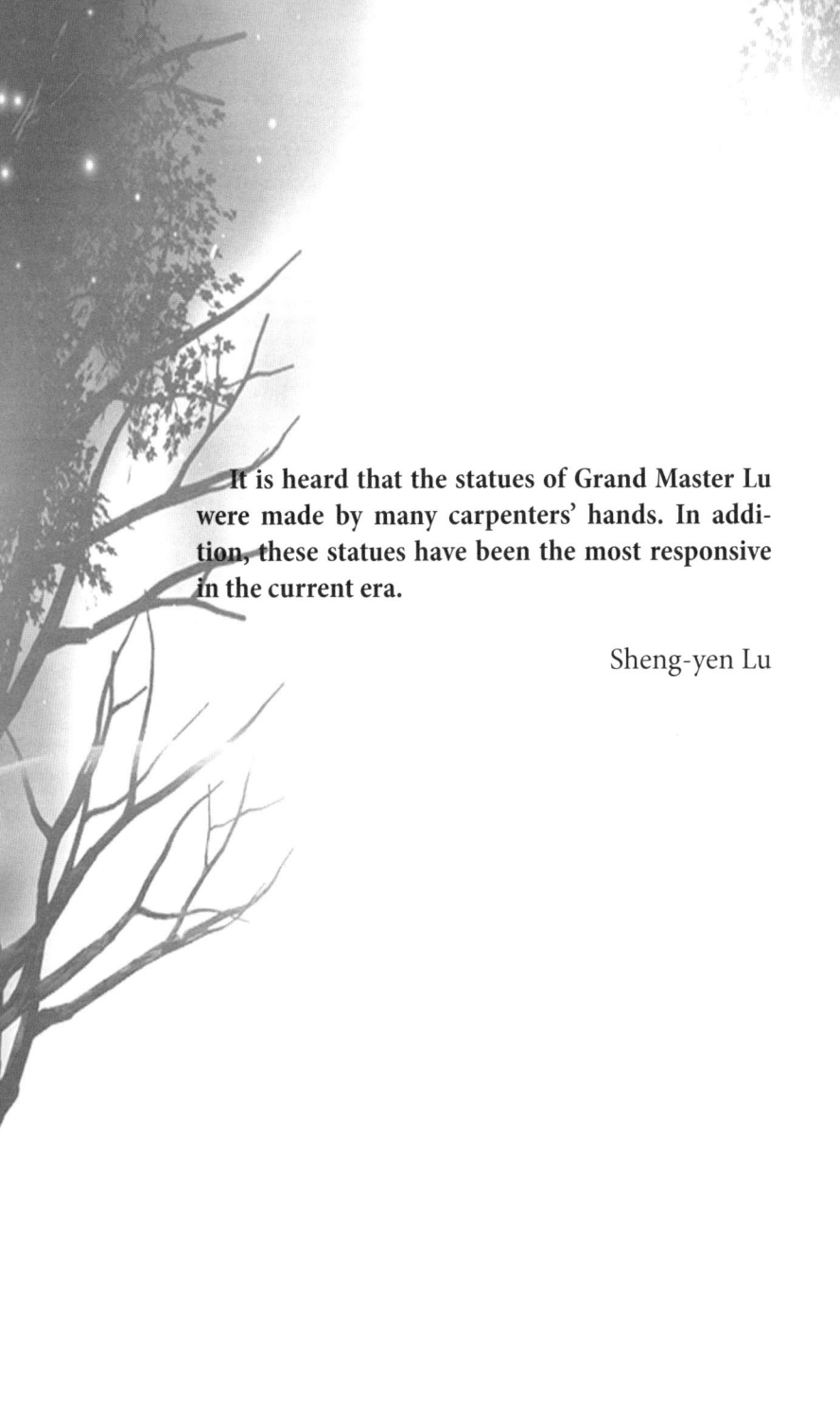

It is heard that the statues of Grand Master Lu were made by many carpenters' hands. In addition, these statues have been the most responsive in the current era.

Sheng-yen Lu

33. Tanzhe Temple

On one of the many mountains located in the Tougou District, Xijiao Gate, Peking, China, there was a Tanzhe Temple.

The temple was built in the Xi Jin Dynasty. At first, it was named Jiafu Temple. It then changed to Longquan Temple in the Ming Dynasty. Later, the name changed again to Wanshou Temple, and Xiuyun Temple.

At last, because there was a pond of "Dragon Tan" in the back hill of the temple, and a silkworm thorn tree of "Zhe tree" at the foothill, therefore, it was renamed formally "Tanzhe Temple."

Why did I write about the Tanzhe Temple?

It was because one of my disciples, Wang Mingda, was surprised to notice, "Padmakumara was among the statues" when visiting the Tanzhe Temple during a tour of China.

The recognition was very obvious. His hands were in the familiar reverse-grip position holding the vajra bell and scepter. Only Padmakumara holds a bell and a scepter in this "reverse-grip" way.

He asked monks there, "Who is the deity?"

The monk replied, "He is the embodiment of five direction Buddhas."

***

How was Padmakumara (Grand Master Lu) in the Tanzhe Temple? No one knew.

I consulted *The Divine Book*.

It stated, "An inspiration of a carpenter."

I took a trip to the Tanzhe Temple in my illusory body and consulted Avalokitesvara Bodhisattva. What Avalokitesvara Bodhisattva told me was that:

"There was a carpenter whose name was Yixiu. He developed a strange sickness. Both legs could not walk.

One day, in his dream, a god appeared and directed him, 'If you wish to cure your legs you must quickly carve an embodiment of five Buddhas. Your legs will recover once it is complete.'

The carpenter asked, 'What does the embodiment of five Buddhas look like?'

The deity described, 'The embodiment of five Buddhas is the Grand Master Lu of current era. His statue holds a vajra bell and a vajra scepter. The most distinguishable thing is that they are held in reverse-grip mudra.'

The deity transformed into the dharma form of Padmakumara (Grand Master Lu) for Yixiu to see.

The Carpenter Yixiu looked and felt it was very unique, because he had never seen any Buddha statues in reverse-grip mudra.

The carpenter therefore finished the embodiment statue of the five-Buddha and completed his promise at the Tanzhe Temple.

Strangely, after he finished the statue of Padmakumara, the legs of the carpenter Yixiu recovered automatically and he was able to walk fast."

I recently found out that, while my illusory body was out traveling in China, I saw many temples all worshiping the statue of Padmakumara (Grand Master Lu.) It is heard that the statues of Grand Master

Lu were made by many carpenters' hands. In addition, the statue has been the most responsive in the current era.

I look forward to someone going to China who will visit the Tan-zhe Temple, and pay homage to the embodiment of five Buddhas, "Padmakumara" (Grand Master Lu), located amongst the statues. Pay attention because this statue can also be found in other temples.

Poem:

The mind of heaven is so ingenious.
The statue is like a gust of wind
However, responses are greatly effective.
Illusory body is like a flying owl?

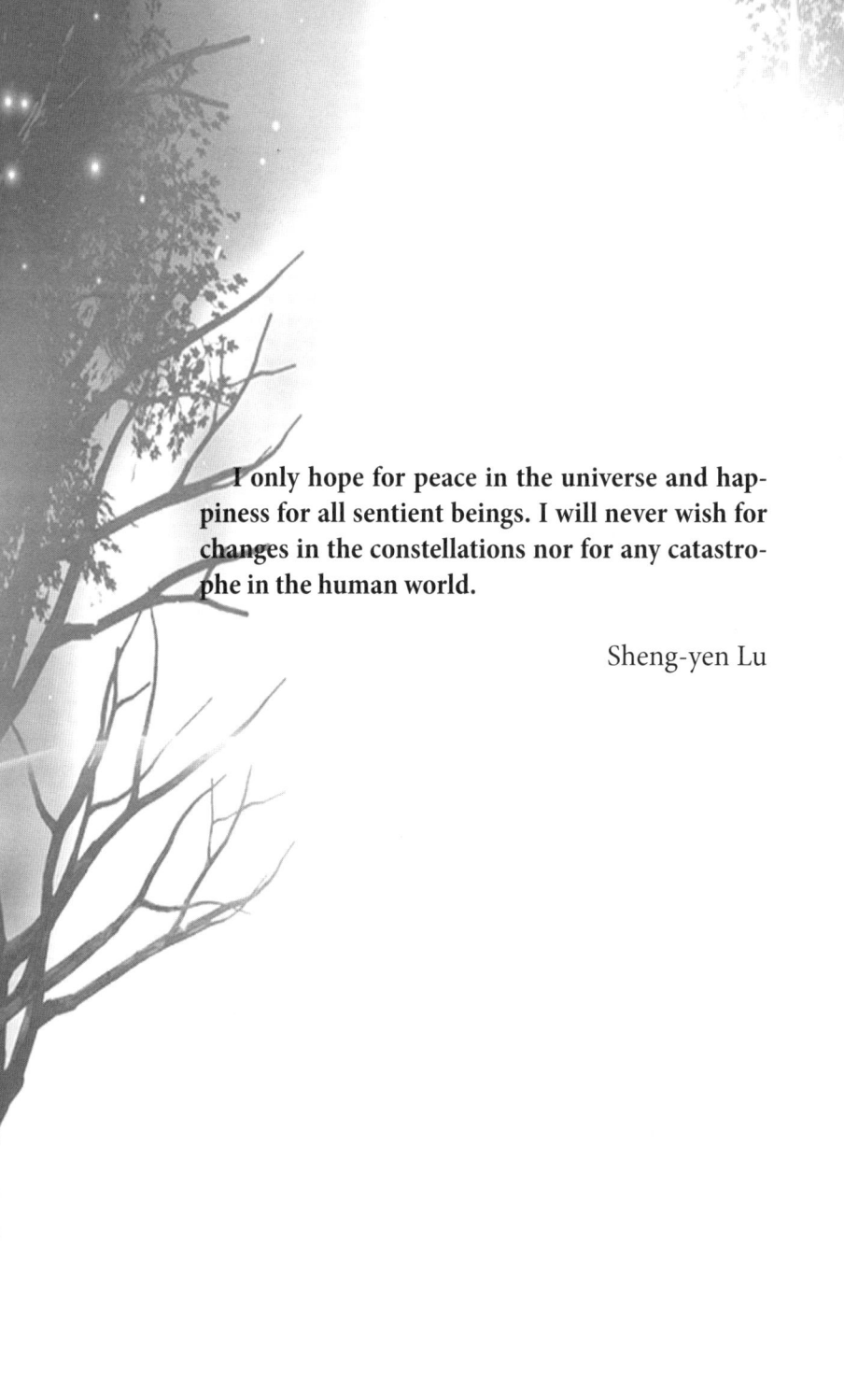

I only hope for peace in the universe and happiness for all sentient beings. I will never wish for changes in the constellations nor for any catastrophe in the human world.

Sheng-yen Lu

34. The Deity of Nine Planets

Once while in my "illusory body," I encountered the Deity of Nine Planets. The deity told me that he was master of the constellations and knew the secrets of the entire universe.

I asked him, "What are the secrets of the constellations?"

He replied, "The constellations never move out of orbit. If they ever veers off course it would cause the catastrophe of the century."

I asked him, "Is there any association between humans and the constellations?"

He replied, "Every human being similarly has their own orbit of fate and it is meant to be unchangeable. It is just like the orbit of the constellations that does not change. However, if it does change, it will bring either great fortune or ill-fate."

I asked him, "This is fate?"

He replied, "Yes it is."

The Deity of Nine Planets then said to me, "Grand Master Lu, your level of practice has already reached the unsurpassed level. You and the constellations are one. You are the constellations and the constellations are you. The movement of one hair can affect the entire body. That is why you are able to command the wind and demand rain."

I replied, "If this is true then it is terrifying. I am simply a common guy who has no desire to change the stars."

The Deity of Nine Planets said, "A practitioner having reached the utmost level becomes joined with the universe. It is not up to you."

I replied, "I am unwilling to be a guilty one. I only hope for peace in the universe and happiness for all sentient beings. I will never wish for changes in the constellations nor for any catastrophe in the human world."

The Deity of Nine Planets merely smiled!

***

Reverend Zhen told me that she had secretly kept records. Every time I was slandered significantly, coincidently, a catastrophe occurred somewhere in the world:

First huge slander - the World Trade Center Tower was hit.
Second huge slander - South Sea Tsunami.
Third huge slander - a severe storm.
Fourth huge slander - the Wenchuan earthquake.

I told Reverend Zhen, "There was absolutely no such thing. I am only the small Sheng-yen Lu, who is compassionate about sentient beings. Saving people is my responsibility. I am already worried that I am out of time. Those events surely had nothing to do with me!"

I pray:

In the human saha world, may everyone be peaceful, happy, and wealthy. May weather be favorable. May the country be prosperous and people be safe.

In the human saha world, may the earth never shake, waters never flood, volcanoes never erupt, and wind and seas always be calm.

In the human saha world, may all four seasons be like spring, climates always be gentle, crops always abundant, and free of calamities.

I consulted *The Divine Book* and asked, "Why do so many disasters

occur in the human world?"
Only one character appeared, "Coincidences."

Poem:

When uniting humans and the universe.
Remarkable abilities come lightly.
Merely raise a vajra scepter.
And the constellations are directed.

It was nothing. This is what a spiritual response is about.

Sheng-yen Lu

35. Never Descend to Four Births

One morning, while sitting for a moment quietly after finishing my early practice, I was surprised to see five characters appear in *The Divine Book*. The five characters were: "Never descend to Four Births."

I did not understand. What was the meaning of the appearance of the five characters, "Never descend to Four Births" in *The Divine Book*?

After performing finger-flexing divination, I learned that if I:

1. Write the five characters down with a Chinese calligraphy brush.
2. Then place the characters on the divination desk.
3. I will then receive a spiritual response.

That same afternoon, I was visited by Mr. Ho Chong who came looking for me in a hurry.

With a sad face, he told me, "My mom, Mrs. Zhu, passed away six months ago. She suddenly appeared in my dream and said, because of the bad karma carried out while living, she was experiencing a bitter existence in the netherworld. Once her suffering there ends, she will then descend further into the animal realm. She is well aware that, in the animal realm she will also suffer extreme torture."

"My mother Mrs. Zhu desperately begged the king of hell not to relegate her to the animal realm. The king of hell was unwilling to promise her anything initially. But after hearing her sad requests multiple times, the king of hell eventually said to her that, your son, Mr. Ho Chong, is a disciple of Grand Master Lu in the upper realm. Grand Master Lu is the contemporary teacher of human and heavenly beings. Only a decree from Grand Master Lu can save you."

"My mother asked the king of hell how will Grand Master Lu save me? The king of hell told her to ask Grand Master Lu to write the five characters 'Never Descend to Four Births.'"

"The five characters are a decree. Burn the decree together with joss paper. Once we receive this decree you will not need to descend to the Four Births. The Four Births are birth from womb, birth by transformation, birth from egg, and birth from moisture. By following this process, you will then be able to ascend to the heavenly realm."

Ho Chong said, "My coming here urgently today is to request Grand Master Lu to write the five characters of 'Never Descend to Four Births.'"

I took out the five characters, "Never Descend to Four Births" pre-written some time ago.

I asked Ho Chong, "Are these the five characters?"

Ho Chong was greatly astonished,

"These are indeed the five characters. Grand Master Lu is so divine. You already foresaw this!"

Ho Chong was very pleasantly surprised.

I smiled lightly and said, "It was nothing. This is what a spiritual response is about."

I told Ho Chong, "Since you want to get rid of your mother's karma, why not chant the Seven Buddha Karma-Exterminating Mantra.

You can also chant Ksitigarbha Bodhisattva Karma-Eliminating Mantra, or Rebirth Mantra. They will all greatly benefit your mother. Go and dedicate them to your mom!"

I also told Ho Chong, "Print and donate the *Guanyin Sutra*, *True Buddha Sutra*, *Diamond Sutra*, and *Taishang Response Sutra*; these will also help to reduce your mother's bad karma. Go and do this right away!"

After returning, Ho Chong carried out everything he had been instructed to do.

One day, Ho Chong came back to inform me, "My mother Mrs. Zhu has indeed been saved. She appeared in my dream wearing a heavenly crown; she was covered with a celestial garment and descended with rainbow radiance surrounding her. She asked me to come and thank Grand Master Lu deeply. The five characters from Grand Master Lu, 'Never Descend to Four Births,' really were a huge decree!"

I smiled lightly, "This was an honor from the king of hell!"

Poem:

Why not practice virtuous deeds,
So one will not suffer a great deal.
The king of hell's laws are strict,
When the lost ones return.

Once the request passed through Grand Master Lu, three months worth of treatment was accomplished in one night.

Sheng-yen Lu

36. Red-eyes

In July, 2008, I took a trip to Austria, Germany, and Switzerland with a group of thirty-three people.

Lady Chen Chuanfang, who enjoys making jokes, as soon as we met, told me,

"Grand Master Lu, from May to July of this year, for the entire three months, my eyes have been constantly red and I do not understand why. These red-eye symptoms are not a serious illness however, it does not feel comfortable. When people see my red eyes they ask me what happened?"

Chen Chuanfang said that she had had "five doctors" examine them, and all five told her that she would recover.

However, two months passed; and her red-eye symptoms never went away.

Chen Chuanfang then asked me to bless her.

I said fine.

A day after my saying "fine" to her, Chen Chuanfang's red-eye symptom truly became fine.

"Five eye specialists had treated her for two months but in vain!"

"Grand Master Lu simply called out one word 'fine' and the very

next day her pinkeye faded away and was cured!"
(Everyone was in awe and expressed their praise.)

***

Actually it was really nothing. That same night, while in practice, I invoked Avalokitesvara Bodhisattva and asked,
"What happened to Chen Chuanfang?"
The Bodhisattva replied, "Her ocular blood vessels are inflamed from a blockage."
"Why were the doctors unable to cure them?"
The Bodhisattva answered, "The doctors treated the inflammation on the surface which did not remove the blockage."
"How can I save her?"
The Bodhisattva responded, "I will use willow tree branches with pure water to wash off her blockage. The eyes will recover the next day!"
I thanked the Bodhisattva, "I thank Avalokitesvara Bodhisattva for her compassion!"
The Bodhisattva said, "Grand Master Lu don't be so polite. A piece of your eye talisman can cure it also. The effect is the same. Since you invoked me to help you I am helping you just this time."
The Bodhisattva then left for Chen Chuanfang!
Once the request passed through Grand Master Lu, three months worth of treatment was accomplished in one night.
Dear readers, can you believe this?
If not, go and ask Chen Chuanfang, the Queen of Jokes in California, USA.

***

During the trip to Europe, I heard about a "Typhoon that was invading Taiwan." My heart was torn with anxiety. I thought about finding the God of Wind.

I opened and consulted *The Divine Book*. It said, "You saved Taiwan before. Once is enough! For any remaining times, let them suffer from their own actions!"

I was disappointed!

With my whole heart I wanted to save Taiwan from the calamity. Unfortunately, they occurred one after another.

Who can tell my true heart? What else could have been done?

Poem:

> *Grievances accumulated in Taiwan,*
> *Feeling torn when thinking about it.*
> *Sentient beings don't blame me,*
> *For raising myself on the pedestal.*

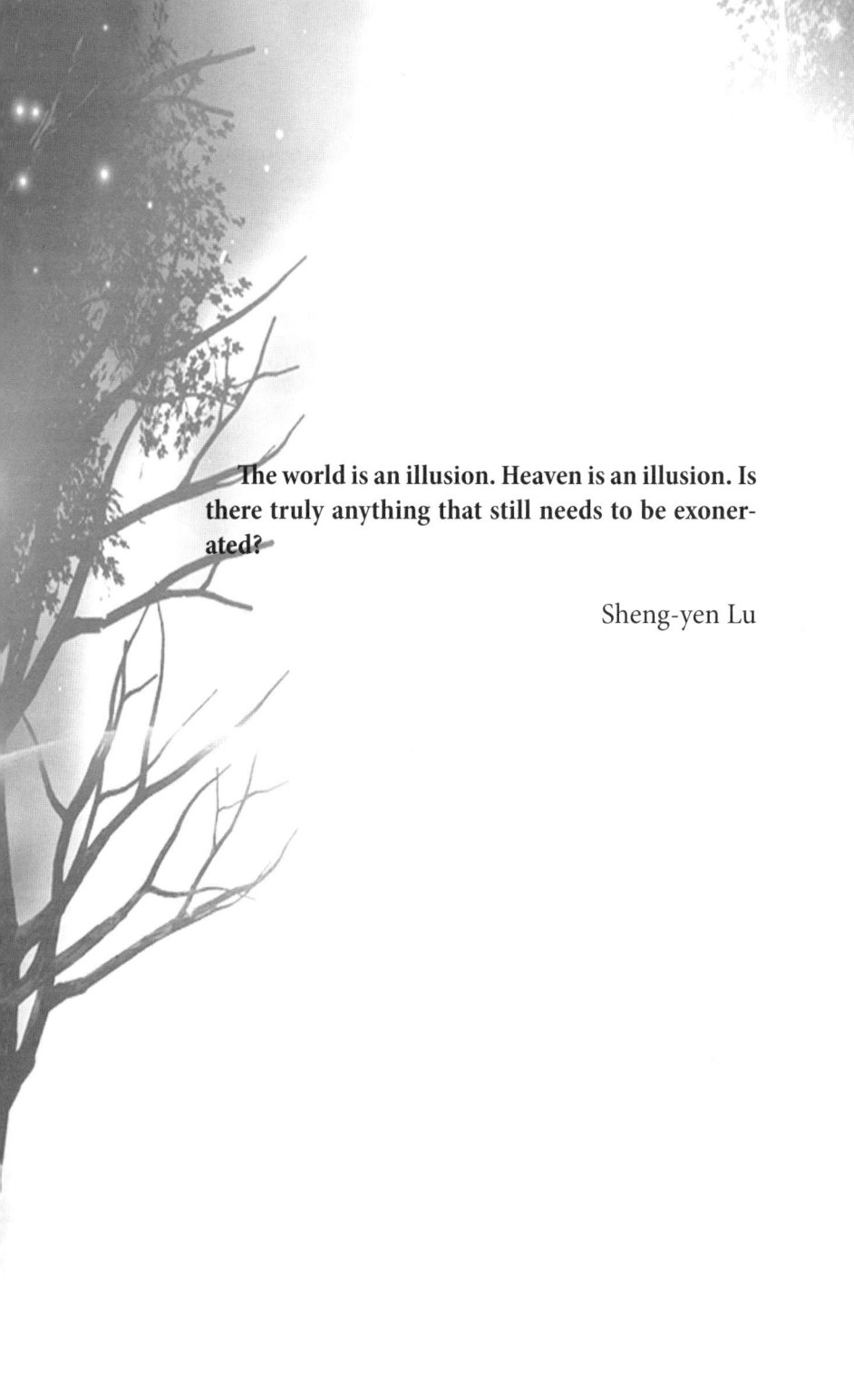

The world is an illusion. Heaven is an illusion. Is there truly anything that still needs to be exonerated?

Sheng-yen Lu

37. The Queen of Indra

Once while in my illusory body, a celestial official came to see me.

The heavenly official said, "The Queen of Indra invites Grand Master Lu to visit her!"

I therefore followed the angelic official and entered the Indra's City of Shanjian.

The City of Shanjian was so spectacular that it still moves me.

Five main altar towers stood tall and upright.

They looked like five mountains.

Just like five fingers.

They were so high that one could not see the top.

The Queen of Indra, Madam Shezhi, wearing a special celestial garment, a phoenix crown, and rainbow cap, stepped down to welcome me.

The queen said,

"Grand Master Lu, I have been slandered by human beings. Therefore, I have brought you here specifically to ask you to straighten out the facts for me."

I asked, "What is the slander?"

The Queen Madam Shezhi, answered, "For one, people in the world think that it was me who incited war between Indra and Ashrah."

"Two, people think that I was the wife of Ashrah. That is not true. People think that Indra possessed the wife of Ashrah because of my beauty."

"Three, people think that my first son is the child of Ashrah. This is false. He is really the child of Indra."

After listening to her, I maintained my composure and asked the Queen Madam Shezhi, "How do you want me to exonerate you from the blame?"

Queen Shezhi replied,

"Write in your book that it started because I was the most beautiful woman of Ashrah and admired Indra. Indra recognized my beauty and married me. Everything else has no basis."

I was silent after hearing what she said.

"Are you not able to clear it for me?"

I consulted *The Divine Book* internally.

In it was written:

> Exoneration will be in vain.
> It is not needed to clear this.
> It is not an issue to begin with.
> Self nature is already pure and clean.

I told Madam Shezhi, "These kind of heavenly stories of Indra, Indra's Queen, and Ashrah's King have been passed down for long time since ancient times. Everyone already knows about them. How can it be possible, by only my, Grand Master Lu's, one word, would able to vindicate happenings in the heavenly realm? Am I not overestimating myself? Therefore, I cannot follow your order and execute the command."

Madam Shezhi replied, "Then it will be forever unjust and wrong."

I replied, "Whether unfair or not just, you must take refuge in the Three Jewels, truly cultivate Buddhism, comprehend the true Buddha nature, and obtain the prajna wisdom of Tathagata. The world is an illusion. Heaven is an illusion. Is there truly anything that still needs to be exonerated?"

Madam Shezhi listened, deeply understood, and responded, "Thus far... I will then take refuge in Grand Master Lu!"

I said, "Do not discard any human beings."

At last, the Queen of the Indra, Madam Shezhi, at the City of Shanjian, took refuge under in Living Buddha Lian-sheng Sheng-yen Lu.

Poem:

Slandering is endless.
Even celestials sigh.
Once one understands non-issue to start with.
No need to pay any attention.

People that are not benevolent are benevolent.

Sheng-yen Lu

38. The Vajra Throne

It has been said that bardo spirits (souls) are not allowed to be in two places:
One is: Buddha's Vajra Throne.
The second is: a woman's womb.
As far as I know, Buddha's Vajra Throne has an inconceivable "boundary protection." In other words, it is inconceivably illusory. It is produced from the Dharma of all illusive wisdom.
All Buddhas and Bodhisattvas respect the Vajra Throne as much as Buddha himself. Therefore, only Buddha can sit on the Vajra Throne. It is unheard of for anybody else to be able to sit on it.
In addition, a woman's womb is a place that only bears someone who has affinity with the woman. It has "affinity" boundary protection.
All bardo spirits, unless having affinity, will not be able to enter the womb.
Although bardo spirits have supernatural powers, they cannot come close to the Vajra Throne or a woman's womb. This is because of the great boundary protection.
I exited in my illusory body, and the King of Vajra appeared from

the illusory body; the King is the supreme, purest, most perfect, and most imperishable of all.

My illusory body not only entered the protective boundary of the Vajra Throne, but also went straight to the front of the Vajra Throne.

This had never happened before.

From ancient times until now, no one has ever made it to the front of the Vajra Throne.

The Bodhisattva of Great Strength questioned me, "Grand Master Lu, how did you get inside the Vajra Throne's protective boundary?"

I replied:

"Absolute and unmovable.

Equal and solid.

Compassion for sentient beings in samsara.

Not being contaminated by forms.

Detached from the three realms."

After hearing this, the Bodhisattva was filled with respect.

***

The Buddha appeared from the Vajra Throne after witnessing my entrance into the protective boundary of the Vajra Throne.

The Buddha said, "Why don't I yield the Vajra Throne for Grand Master Lu to sit on?"

I replied, "Buddhas of three generations all respect the Buddha and acknowledge that the Vajra Throne only belongs to Buddha. No one dares take the seat, and neither do I, Grand Master Lu."

The Buddha said, "Take a seat, do not mind!"

I hesitated thinking to myself. The Buddha sincerely invited me. If I did not take the seat, would I be disobeying the Buddha's will?

As I was hesitating, the following words appeared in *The Divine Book*:

Over the Vajra Throne of the Buddha,
appears the Vajra Dharma canopy;
It is the manifestation of the Buddha's body and mind.
It is disrespectful if you sit in it.

After seeing this I clearly understood.

I answered, "I am capable of entering the Dharma boundary of the Vajra Throne, because I possess the treasure of vajra, have attained confusion-breaking wisdom, terminating even the most subtle ignorance. Therefore, it is equivalent to enlightenment."

"However, I cannot take a seat on the Vajra Throne, because it is the body and mind of the Buddha. Buddha's body and mind are the head of vajra. How can I sit on it?"

Buddha asked, "Grand Master Lu, why are the benevolent not benevolent?"

I replied, "People that are not benevolent are benevolent."

Poem:

Not to sit on the vajra throne.
One is still a vajra.
Buddhas exist in the ten directions,
Not because they sit or do not to sit.

I am being totally honest when I tell everyone that, my enlightenment is absolute. It is beyond power, beyond worldly treasures, beyond fame, beyond material objects, and beyond desires.

Sheng-yen Lu

39. Enlightened as Buddha's Enlightenment

One day I became enlightened. I looked up enlightenment in *The Divine Book* and in it was written "Enlightened as Buddha's enlightenment" meaning that what I comprehended was exactly the same as what Shakyamuni Buddha did when he became enlightened under the Bodhi tree.

It was indeed the "Enlightenment of Buddha's enlightenment."
After I became enlightened, I could:
    See through life and death.
    See through worries.
    See through illusions.
    See through existence.
    See through emptiness.
    Even see through the universe.
    And so on and so forth.
Of course I understand what is the great wisdom mantra, the great spiritual mantra, the surpassed mantra, and unequaled mantra.

The comprehension is "supreme," therefore it is also referred to as "unsurpassed perfect enlightenment."

Of course I understand what is:

Form emptiness.
Mind emptiness.
Dharma emptiness.
Nature emptiness.
Being enlightened, naturally this is how it is, this is how it is.

But I still question how a sage such as Confucius could have back then made the statement, "If having heard the path in the morning, one can die that night!" Could it be that Confucius also had come to realize what Buddha did? (This enlightenment is difficult for worldly people to understand.)

Ever since I obtained the Seal of Buddha's mind, I have known what "this" is!

I myself know that no other awareness exists beyond "this." Nothing else is more precious than "this." Nothing else is more valuable than "this." With "this," tangible objects of the world are all diminished.

Space, time, tangibles, and intangibles of the world will all be gone. This is a state of complete nirvana.

In regards to:
  Power,
  Assets,
  Fame,
  Material,
  Desires,
I could only cry out, "Oh, heaven!, Oh, heaven!"

My whole life and fame have been shattered completely resulting in no fame at all. Again I could only cry out, "Oh, heaven!, Oh, heaven!"

I am being totally honest when I tell everyone that, my enlightenment is absolute. It is beyond power, beyond worldly treasures, beyond fame, beyond material objects, and beyond desires.

Even beyond:
  "Reincarnation"

"Nirvana."

Of course I cannot simply publically announce what "Enlightened as Buddha's enlightenment" is in a book, or even disclose it in my Dharma talks. This is because everyone's ability of being awakened is at a different level.

If one is on the verge of reaching enlightenment, then one will be enlightened in a second.

If one is not yet close to being awakened, adversely, one will defame instead.

Therefore, this is why "I cannot tell! I cannot tell!"

Poem:

> *What can I complain about in this life.*
> *I am already standing on the peak.*
> *I am enlightened with the great Enlightenment of the Buddha.*
> *See through life's emptiness and illusions.*

I of course understand that the boundaries of the ten realms of four enlightened and six unenlightened are all naturally "protected."

Sheng-yen Lu

40. Three Little Black Dogs

It was in a middle of a group cultivation on Saturday, July 26, 2008. I momentarily closed my eyes due to jet lag, having just returned to Seattle, United States, from Europe.

Unexpectedly I saw a group of people fleeing from their homeland. Moreover, I also saw three little black dogs.

The three little black dogs were standing on a bridge post, panicking like ants in a hot pen.

They were panicking because the water under the bridge had gradually risen to the top of the post. The current was rapid. Rain was heavy and pouring down. The water had risen so quickly that soon it would be drowning the three little black dogs.

I consulted *The Divine Book* and written there I saw:

Two characters, "Protect the Boundary."

With all my Dharma power, I built a "protective boundary" around the refugees from the homeland and the three little black dogs.

The "protective boundary" was:

An intangible shelter formed of energy.

It covered the people and the three little black dogs.

Because the three little dogs were inside the intangible dome of energy, they were able to float on the water, and were not likely to drown.

Emerging from my meditation, I mentioned to the disciples at the group cultivation that, "I saw a group of refugees and black dogs..."

***

Later, I understood: What had happened was that a large typhoon was landing in Taiwan again. The name of the typhoon was "Phoenix."

It landed from the east and continued moving towards the ocean from Zhanghua.

It was a medium strength typhoon.

Yet the wind speed was as high as level seventeen.

It had a radius of two hundred miles.

And was accompanied by torrential rains.

It flooded many cities and towns in Taiwan, even submerging bridges.

It turned out that the story of the three little dogs had really happened. Television stations had recorded the three little dogs on a bridge post.

Later, when the water level rose, the footage lost sight of the three little dogs.

After the typhoon passed, footage of the bridge post showed again, but the three little dogs had long gone.

Oddly enough, the three little black dogs were neither drowned by the high water nor flushed out into the ocean by rapid currents. On the contrary, they appeared later relaxing on the rivershore. They had a great destiny.

I happily watched this unfold.

It turned out that the "protective boundary" had significant benefits:

1. Vajrayana practitioners can protect themselves with it.

2. It can be used to avoid calamities.
3. To dodge earth, water, fire, and wind.
4. To guard one's own life.
5. To shield oneself from any invasion by foreign spirits.
6. No matter how large the country or family, or how small the personal altar or individual, all can be boundary protected.

I of course understand that the boundaries of the ten realms of four enlightened and six unenlightened are all naturally "protected."

Poem:

Buddhist Dharma is truly convenient.
It is able to save one from all calamities.
One finger-pointing covers all.
Darkness turns into brilliance.

"How about your desire, Bodhisattva Sheng-yen?" I answered, "It is a game."

Sheng-yen Lu

41. Discussion of Desire With Fengfeng

I met with Fengfeng while in meditation. I mentioned that I had read many of his books, such as *Dawn,* one of his earlier works, to later ones such as:
Void Cloud,
The Experience of The Divine Eye and Meditation,
Proof of Buddhism with Space Science and Nuclear Physics,
Siddhartha.
....
Every time Fengfeng gave me a book, he wrote on an empty page: "Bodhisattva Sheng-yen, please review this.
Presented with respect, Fengfeng 1984-1 1"
In fact, instead of putting his books away high in the cabinet, I finished reading all of them.

Fengfeng was very surprised and exclaimed when he heard that I had read all his books. He said, "It has been said since ancient times that literati are inclined to despise one another, but this is not the case for Bodhisattva Sheng-yen, Grand Master Lu. I did not expect you to read all my books!"

I smiled and said, "Actually, not only your books, but I have also read books by Master Xingyun, Master Shengyan, Master Zhengyan, Buddhist Monk Miaolian, and even Layman Xiao Pingshi. I have read them all. With regard to the books of Layman Chen Huijian, who criticized and hurt me the most, I read all of them too."

Layman Fengfeng said, "I cannot be compared to you. I disdain some books, especially those that criticize me. So much so that I grunted with contempt.'"

I laughed loudly, "It is good to read."

Fengfeng said, "What is your evaluation of *Siddhartha*, a book that I translated from Hermann Hesse?"

I answered, "That is a book about the recurrence, cessation, and revolution of flowing forms.

Fengfeng said, "Yes, yes, yes. It constantly varies. It exists momentarily, then thousands of changes appear.'"

I asked Fengfeng, "Do you have any desire?"

Fengfeng answered, "All sentient beings do. Shouldn't I?"

I said, "I like your poem."

> *Beauties return to the forest of Phoenix.*
> *Monks stop at the edge of a holy path.*
> *Lotuses emerging from mud are voluptuous.*
> *Monks cultivate Buddhism reverently.*
> *Once I see beauties' smile,*
> *My zen heart transforms to a worldly one.*
> *Cultivating diligently and taking refuge in Buddha,*
> *Cannot compete with worshiping a beauty.*

Fengfeng said, "The inspiration came from the love songs of the Sixth Dalai Lama. The Sixth Dalai Lama's love songs were really truthful."

His Holiness, the Sixth Dalai Lama's love songs:

> *On top of the eastern hill,*
> *Rises a bright and clear moon.*
> *The face of the beautiful girl,*
> *Appears in my heart.*

Another one:

> *Quietly meditating on the master's face,*
> *No matter it did not appear.*
> *It is a lover's face,*
> *That unexpectedly arises from my heart vividly.*

And one more:

> *Meeting a lover after darkness falls,*
> *Snow falling when at the break of dawn.*
> *Footprints imprinted in the snow.*
> *What then is the use of keeping it secret?*

Fengfeng said, "The desire of the Sixth Dalai Lama drove him to write hundreds of love poems."

I asked Fengfeng, "How about your desire?"

Fengfeng answered honestly, "Desire is the source of my motivation to write."

Fengfeng asked me in return, "How about your desire, Bodhisattva Sheng-yen?"

I answered, "It is a game."

Poem:

Flowers blossom then wither away.
Lovers age from young to old.
Only the pure of heart,
Hasten and take refuge.

42. Copper Body Iron Bone Talisman

Shimu, "Master Lianxiang" turned sixty this year, and I turned sixty-four; we are four years apart in age.

Based on the results of her physical exams, she is relatively healthy, except for osteoporosis.

In 2005, after undergoing a thorough medical and diagnostics, her bone density was determined to be below the lower limit index.

Another full physical conducted in 2007 revealed that her bone density had decreased much further to the dangerous level.

Dr. Xiao said, "Treat it without delay!"

Dr. Zhang said, "Take calcium supplements immediately!"

Unfortunately, all medicines prescribed by the family doctors upset Master Lianxiang's stomach.

The family doctors tried all kinds of treatment, including injections, liquid solutions, and patches; but none helped Master Lianxiang who experienced nothing but discomfort from these treatments.

Finally, the doctors exhausted all alternatives and were unable to think of any other solutions.

***

I heard that patients with severe osteoporosis can easily:

1. Break their pelvis from minor falls,
2. Fracture their bones from carrying heavy objects,
3. Crack their bones from simply twisting the body

And so on...

The bones of these patients are no longer strong; they gradually lose density and become porous.

Master Lianxiang had been very concerned about her osteoporosis.

I joked with her, "Not to worry, I will push you around if you are confined to a wheelchair in the future!"

She said, "You will push me into Lake Sammamish!"

Ha, ha, ha!

***

On June 29, 2008, desiring to save Master Lianxiang from the severe illness, I opened *The Divine Book* to find out about a cure.

In *The Divine Book* was written:

"Copper Body Iron Bone Talisman."

That evening, I drew a "Copper Body Iron Bone Talisman" and affixed the paper charm to the side of Master Lianxiang's foot.

The next day, June 30, 2008, Master Lianxiang visited a hospital affiliated with the University of Washington. She was evaluated by the most advanced technology and equipment, and underwent comprehensive tests conducted by Doctor Susan, an osteoporosis specialist.

The results came out, "Master Lianxiang does not have osteoporosis. She is even healthier than the average person. Her bones will have no problem supporting her until she is one hundred years old."

Wow!

We were all astonished!

Diagnosed by two previous physicians, her suffering from osteoporosis was certain, yet the final result was

"Copper Body Iron Bones."

As soon as I, Grand Master Lu's "Copper Body Iron Bone Charm" was applied, it honestly transformed her to a copper body of iron bones!

Poem:

> *Having osteoporosis is really sad.*
> *Slow response, slow pace.*
> *Apply the Copper Body Iron Bone Charm.*
> *Experience rejuvenation, restored youth.*

I have decrees of the Buddha, Golden Mother of the Jade Pond, and the eminent Mr. Three-Peaks Nine-States.

Sheng-yen Lu

43. Typhoon Fengshen

On May 3, 2008, at Linkou Stadium in Taoyuan, Taiwan, I presided over a Kalachakra Ceremony. About thirty thousand people attended the ceremony.

Not long after, in mid-June, a strong tropical storm named Fengshen developed near the Philippines.

According to the weather bureau:

Fengshen had rapidly intensified from a minor tropical depression into a mild tropical cyclone. Later it developed into a severe tropical storm.

It was heading towards the Taiwan Strait from Luzon Island in the Philippines.

Soon the western part of Taiwan, including south and north Taiwan, would be completely under its power.

...

I started hearing comments:

"Fengshen did not honor Grand Master, as it formed just one month after the ceremony."

"A strong typhoon comes soon after the Kalachakra ceremony which shows that the ceremony was powerless. It was totally ineffective."

"Fengshen is an intentional trouble-maker."

"Fengshen swept past Luzon Island which caused serious injuries and casualties to the island. The island was completely bulldozed and severely damaged."

"Fengshen will dominate Taiwan."

***

I was feeling a little despondent.

The Kalachakra ceremony was indeed potent and powerful. Why was there a hurricane just one month after the ceremony?

What could I do to save the place where I grew up?

I consulted *The Divine Book*.

In it was written, "Wind Sky," two characters.

I flew out in my illusory body and advanced towards the northwest, chanting the name of "Wind Sky":

"Fu Yefei! Fu Yefei! Fu Yefei!"

I then saw the Wind-Sky God.

One of five Western celestial gods, the Wind-Sky God has a red-black body and is very tall. His right hand holds a staff, while his left hand rests on his waist. Flags flutter around him.

I asked, "Is Typhoon Fengshen heading for Taiwan?"

Wind-Sky God replied, "Yes."

I asked again, "Can it be averted?"

"No."

"So you are not giving my ceremony any respect?"

The Wind-Sky God answered, "Heaven, earth, thunder, wind, lakes, water, fire and mountains all carry out orders of Sakra, which cannot be disobeyed."

I said, "But I have decrees of the Buddha, Golden Mother of the Jade Pond, and the eminent Mr. Three-Peaks Nine-States. Is that not enough?"

Astounded by what I said, the Wind-Sky God then secretly told me, "Please perform a Wind-Sky ritual and the problem will be solved." (However, the ritual can only be performed once a year.)

I placed a lit candle at the seed syllable HA in the southwest corner of the mandala, performed the ritual, and then blew out the flame.

Strangely enough, Fengshen soon weakened into a tropical depression after hitting Luzon Island. It then dissipated and disappeared.

Poem:

> *Fengshen is like a vicious woman,*
> *Whereas I am a teacher of men and the heavens,*
> *By the higher mandate of immense urgency,*
> *Fengshen's eye is blown away.*

Exiting in my illusory body, I searched from the highest to the lower realms.

Sheng-yen Lu

44. Search for Zheng Cheng Gong

Once a disciple from Tainan, Taiwan, asked me a question in a letter. The disciple said, "Zheng Cheng Gong is the Deity Yanping Junwang, who dwelt in the Chikan Mansion. He defeated the Dutch to recover Taiwan. I would like to ask Grand Master, which realm did Zheng Cheng Gong reincarnate to?"

Zheng Cheng Gong was the son of Zheng Zhi Long, the father of Zheng Jing, and the grandfather of Zheng Ke Shuang. Zheng Cheng Gong is the hero who recovered Taiwan. I thought it should not be difficult to trace the reincarnation of Zheng Cheng Gong. I did not meditate deeper to consult *The Divine Book*, instead I used my illusory body to search for Zheng Cheng Gong.

Exiting in my illusory body, I searched from the highest to the lower realms. Starting from the Four Holy Realms of Buddha, Bodhisattva, PratyekaBuddha and Sravaka, I could not find Zheng Cheng Gong.

I went to the Formless Realm, but was unable to find Zheng Cheng Gong.

I went to the Form Realm, again failing to find Zheng Cheng Gong.
I went to the Desire Realm, even in there I could not find him.

This made me feel very strange.
I continued to search in the Deity Realms:
 Dragon King Realm,
 Yakṣa King Realm,
 Asura King Realm,
 Golden-Winged Garuda King Realm,
 Raksa King Realm,
 Earth, Water, Fire, Wind Deity Realm,
 Thunder Deity Realm,
 Etc.
The result was unexpected. Even in the Deity Realms I found no trace of Zheng Cheng Gong (the Deity Yanping Junwang).

I then searched among the "Earth-Based Deities", these included Town Deities, Lot Deities, Land Deities, Mountain Deities, River Deities, Lake Deities …

Still I found no hint of Zheng Cheng Gong.

By then, I was anxious and wondered if Zheng was hidden among the Territorial Deities, such as the Sacred Prince, Founder of Zhangzhou, the Five Dukes, Saintly Mother of the Sky, Three Mountain Kings, and so on.

Since the Deity Yan Ping Jun Wang is a Territorial Deity, I was so sure this time that I would find him.

However, I still did not.

Running out of ideas, I eventually used my illusory body to look into the Fairy Realms, such as the Children's Fairy, People's Fairy, Responsive Fairy, Mighty Virtuous Fairy, the Honorable Eighteen Kings, and the Honorable Significant Public Mother.

I couldn't find him there either.

I almost despaired. From the highest realms down to the Fairy Realms, there was not even a shadow of Zheng Cheng Gong. I searched a temple named Taiwan Founding Saint Temple worshipping Zheng Cheng Gong as its main deity. However, it turned out that the deity was not Zheng Cheng Gong. It was one with last name Shi.

This time I thought about the Evil Spirits Realm. Could it be possible that Zheng Cheng Gong became an evil spirit? Zheng Cheng Gong is a national hero, how could he be in the Evil Spirits Realm? This is impossible.

Nonetheless I went ahead and looked. As expected, there was no Zheng Cheng Gong in the Evil Spirits Realm.

I thought that I should be able to find famous Zheng Cheng Gong (the Deity Yanping Junwang) in my illusory body. Surprisingly I could not. At the end and without other choices, I had to meditate deeper to consult *The Divine Book*. In the book it wrote "XX Realm". I was shocked. May I ask you what realm you think this is? Please contemplate it.

Poem:

> *Dim candle light and quiet pedestrians.*
> *Searching for a person in the illusory body.*
> *It is cause and effect.*
> *On and on the regret remains.*

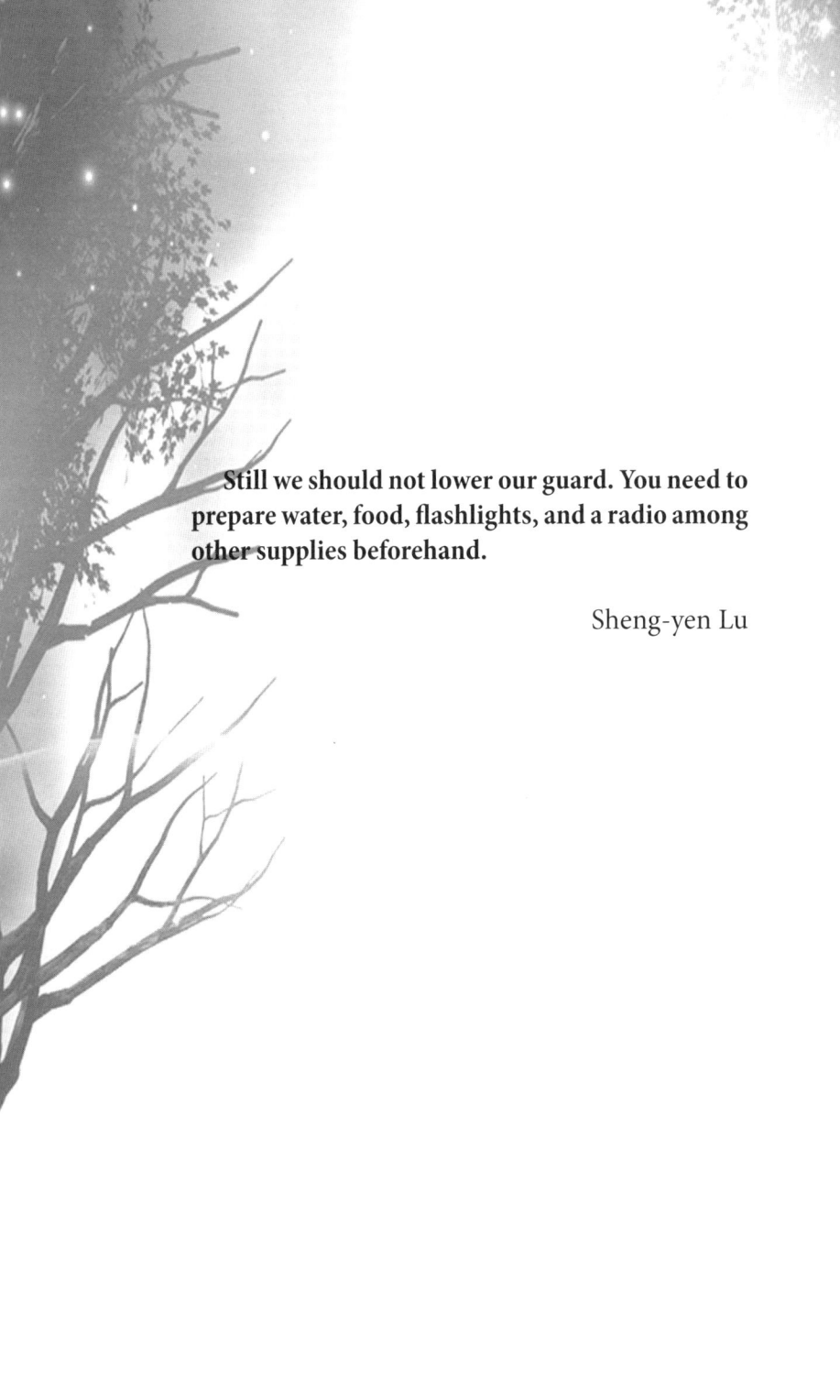

Still we should not lower our guard. You need to prepare water, food, flashlights, and a radio among other supplies beforehand.

Sheng-yen Lu

45. California's Huge Earthquake

While traveling in Europe, I was accompanied by disciples including the "four ladies" from Los Angeles, California, namely Sun Aizhen, Wei Siyan, Chen Chuanfang, and Jiang Guanrong.

News and documentaries constantly warn of a pending huge earthquake in California. These forecasts are neither groundless, nor hearsay, but based on seismology.

California actually sits on a seismic belt consisting of a series of faults where a huge earthquake hit a hundred years ago.

Since then, the earth has accumulated an enormous amount of energy much like the situation a century ago. This energy is so powerful that once released, may create an earthquake with magnitude of nine or ten on the Richter scale.

If an earthquake of this magnitude were to strike, it would result in an unimaginable catastrophe.

The probability of such an earthquake occurring in California is said to be as high as ninety-nine percent.

This is disturbing news and has California residents very concerned.

***

Naturally, the "four ladies" from California were very troubled by the pending huge earthquake. They repeatedly asked me what could be done.

"Will the earthquake strike?"

I answered, "Yes." (*The Divine Book* wrote "yes" too.)

"What should we do?"

I answered, "As we cultivate Buddhadharma, Bodhisattvas and protectors will in turn protect us. At the same time, we must equip ourselves with the know-how to survive an earthquake. This is fundamental."

"Will Grand Master Lu help us?"

I answered, "Of course."

"How do you intend to help?"

I answered, "By reducing major issues to minor ones, and minor ones to nothing. I shall keep you safe and sound."

Chen Chuan-Fang said, "Having Grand Master Lu around, everything will be fine."

I said, "Still we should not lower our guard. You need to prepare water, food, flashlights, and a radio among other supplies beforehand. And you need to arm yourself with the basic knowledge of escape and survival so that when the earthquake hits, you can avert the disaster. In addition to California, Seattle is also seated on a seismic belt, hence those living in Seattle have to be just as alert."

"But Grand Master Lu resides in Seattle, not California."

"I will pray for you."

I prayed as follows: "When the earthquake comes, reduce its magnitude to half from ten; or make it disappear altogether."

***

As expected, an earthquake of 5.4 magnitude struck California. It occured on July 29, 2008 at noon.

People were frightened.

Fortunately, it was a shallow earthquake measuring only 5.4 on the Richter scale.

No serious casualties were reported.

I said, "Regardless, I have the responsibility to watch over my disciples in California. May the power of the boundary protection guard my disciples in California!"

Poem:

> *The city was ruined in the past.*
> *Now a repeat earthquake will strike any time.*
> *I pray to reduce the damage to half.*
> *So that family (disciples) will not part.*

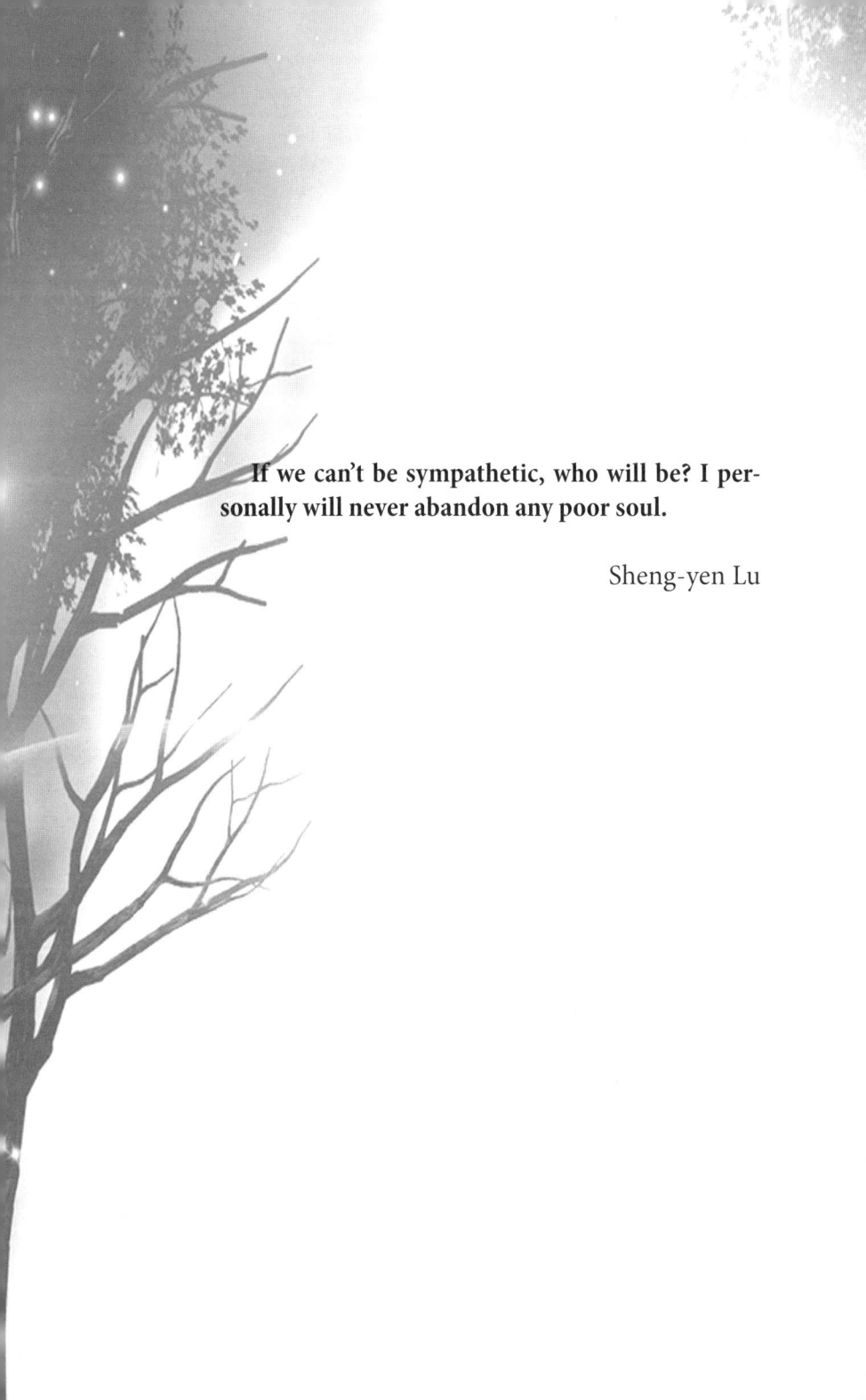

**If we can't be sympathetic, who will be? I personally will never abandon any poor soul.

Sheng-yen Lu

46. I Heard a Woman Cry

One day when I was meditating in the True Buddha Quarter, I unexpectedly heard a woman sobbing in the Temple. Her sobs were sometimes loud and sometimes soft.

After listening more closely, I became convinced that it was from a woman sorrowfully imploring.

Though the Seattle Temple and the True Buddha Quarter are not far apart, it is still impossible to hear sounds from the Quarter to the Temple or vise versa.

I asked my reverends, "Has someone been crying in the temple?"

They looked at me perplexed.

I asked again, "Who was crying in the temple?"

At then, one finally said,

"Recently a woman has been coming to the temple in the afternoon. She often cries to the Buddhas for a while, then sits quietly, and then she laughs under her breath discreetly."

Another added, "We believe she is mentally ill or unstable, so we didn't tell Grand Master Lu about her."

"How long has this been going on?"

"Just these recent weeks."

I said, "As reverends, we should approach and care for her regardless of how she reached that plight, from being ill-treated, sickness, or hardship."

One reverend said, "Due to prior experiences, we didn't dare to inform Grand Master of her presence fearing that she might harm Grand Master. We should avoid anyone who is mentally unstable like her!"

I said, "Buddha is the embodiment of compassion and mercy. It is already unfortunate to be mentally ill. In addition, she might have a lot of resentment towards life. If we can't be sympathetic, who will be? I personally will never abandon any poor soul. We all should help her!"

I asked my reverends to assist and take care of any woman in the same situation.

If she is indeed faced with great difficulties, I will also try my best to help her.

This sad woman was dealing with three big issues:

1. Being single in America without a job.
2. Having two rebellious children.
3. Having no friends or relatives to depend on.

She took refuge in me at the group cultivation on July 26, 2008.

On first seeing her, I consulted *The Divine Book* and knew immediately what she had undergone in life.

A woman cried in the temple and I could even hear it in the True Buddha Quarter.

It was mystical! It was mystical!

What if I hadn't asked and the reverends had kept her presence a secret? Then I would have missed the chance to save her.

I shall fully support and help her.

Poem:

Enlighten all the beings as we cultivate Buddha-nature.
Converting sentient beings is not in name only.
No being will be given up.
This is the real Buddha spirit.

Glossary

-A-

Abhidharma
Also known as the sastras, which are the doctrinal commentaries, philosophical works, discourses, discussions, treatises on the dogma, and doctrines of Buddhism which summarize key points and classify teachings.

Affinity
A relationship by fate or destiny, is a Buddhist-related Chinese concept that means the predetermined principle that dictates a person's relationships and encounters, such as the affinity among family, friends or lovers. In common usage the term can be defined as the "binding force" that links two people together in any relationship. It is also used to explain events occuring at in people's lives. The driving forces and causes behind affinity are created as a result of previous lives.

Amitabha Buddha (Sanskrit, literally "Boundless light")
The Buddha of Boundless Light and Longevity, he is one of the Five Wisdom Buddhas and the Lord of the Lotus Family. He embodies the Wisdom of Discerning Awareness which is the antidote to desire and lust. His color is red, element is fire, and direction is west. He is depicted with his hands forming the meditation mudra. Amitabha Buddha's pure land (paradise) is called Sukhavati and is located in the western direction. He is the Primary Buddha of the Pure Land Sect and often depicted to be accompanied by his two attendants, Avalokitesvara Bodhisattva and Mahasthamaprapta Bodhisattva.

Anatta (Anatman)
Nonself, non ego, nonessentiality; one of the three marks of everything existing, conditioned arising – trilakshana (impermanence, suffering & nonself/egolessness). The Anatta doctrine is one of the central teachings of Buddhism; it states that no self exists in a sense of a permanent, eternal, integral and independent substance within an individual existent. Thus, the ego in Buddhism is no more than a transitory and changeable – and therefore a suffering-prone empirical personality manufactured from the five aggregates (skandas – form, sensation, perception, mental formations and consciousness). In Hinayana, Anatta is limited to the personality; in Mahayana, it is applied to all conditionally arising phenomenon. This freedom from self-nature is called shunyata (emptiness), literally devoid of all existence.

Apsara Deity
A female spirit of the clouds and waters in Hindu and Buddhist mythology. English translations of the word "Apsara" include "nymph," "celestial nymph," and "celestial maiden." Apsaras are beautiful, supernatural female beings. They are youthful and elegant and skilled in the art of dancing. Traditionally they are described as celestial maidens living in Indra's heaven. They are known for their special task of being sent to earth by Indra to seduce ascetics who, through their practices, have become more powerful than the gods.

Arhat (Sanskrit, literally "Worthy One, Vanquisher of Enemies")
One who has exhausted all defilements and mental afflictions that cause one to take rebirth in the six realms of samsara (the cycle of karma and reincarnation), hence is free from suffering and entered into nirvana (the state of liberation from samsara).

Asura (Jealous God)
One of six realms within samsara. Beings in this realm are character-

ized as being very jealous and prone to fighting and arguing with beings in the realm of heaven.

Avalokitesvara (Sanskrit, literally "Lord Who Observes Sounds of the World")
The embodiment of compassion, Avalokitesvara Bodhisattva compassionately observes the sounds of the world and renders assistance to any devotee who calls out his name. The stories of prayers answered and the myriad miracles performed by Avalokitesvara made him the most widely worshipped bodhisattva. Known as Chenrezig in Tibet, the Tibetan people claim to be his descendents and consider him as their patron bodhisattva. They believe that Chenrezig has appeared many times in Tibet to protect the Buddhist faith. King Songtsan Gampo (the Tibetan king who introduced Buddhism into Tibet) and Dalai Lama are believed by Tibetans to be incarnations of Chenrezig. As result of this special relationship, Avalokitesvara's mantra, "Om Mani Padme Hum," is the most widely chanted mantra by the Tibetan people.

Avalokitesvara Bodhisattva is worshipped in China as the female bodhisattva, Guanyin. This change of Avalokitesvara from a male bodhisattva to being depicted as a female one apparently occurred gradually during the Song Dynasty. Some have postulated that Chinese worship Avalokitesvara as a female deity because Chinese culture views compassion as a feminine quality. Guanyin's popularity in China is summed up by the Chinese saying that "The Amitabha Buddha's name is chanted in every house. Guanyin Bodhisattva is worshipped in every home." As Buddhism spread from China into the neighboring Asian countries such as Korea and Japan, Avalokitesvara was introduced to them as Guanyin, a female bodhisattva. The Buddhist scriptures speak of Avalokitesvara appearing in many forms including the two armed, four armed, or the thousand armed and thousand eyed Avalokitesvara. The scriptures also state that Avalokitesvara will appear in the most suitable form for the circum stances when rendering assistance.

-B-

Bodhicitta (Sanskrit, literally "Awakened Mind")
The key to Mahayana Buddhism, it refers both to an enlightened mind and to the resolution arising for the profound compassion to attain an enlightened mind for the purpose of assisting all beings.

Bodhisattva (Sanskrit, literally "Enlightenment-being with Compassion")
One who has developed the altruistic motive of dedicating his existence throughout all rebirths to the attainment of enlightenment in order to liberate other beings who are suffering in samsara (the cycle of karma and reincarnation). In Mahayana Buddhism, there are fifty-two grounds (stages) schemata of enlightenment. It depends on one's merits and virtues, the development of bodhisattva path stands from the forty-first to the fiftieth grounds. Sometimes, it is referring to the "Bodhisattva Path Ten Development Grounds" and they are: (41) Pramudita - joy ground; (42) Vimala - purity ground; (43) Prabhakari - enlightenment ground; (44) Arcismati - wisdom ground; (45) Sudurjaya - no difficulty ground; (46) Abhimukhi - open way ground; (47) Duramgama - proceeding afar ground; (48) Acala - unperturbed ground; (49) Sadhumati - discriminatory wisdom ground; (50) Dharma megha - dharma cloud ground (see Perfect Enlightenment and Wondrous Enlightenment).

Buddha (Sanskrit, literally "Awakened One")
The term is typically used to refer to the historical Buddha, Shakya-

muni Buddha. In Mahayana Buddhism, the term is not restricted to just Shakyamuni Buddha, but may refers to anyone who is enlightened.

Buddhadharma
Buddha doctrine or the teachings of the Buddha.

Buddhahood
The stage of enlightenment.

Buddha-nature
The inherent nature of all sentient beings. All sentient beings have the potential to awaken their buddha-nature and become buddhas.

-C-

Chakravartin
The ancient Indian concept of the world ruler, derived from the Sanskrit chakra "wheel," and vartin, "one who turns." Thus, a Chakravartin may be understood as a world ruler "whose chariot wheels roll everywhere," or "whose movements are unobstructed." Four types of Chakravartin are distinguished and symbolized by wheels of gold, silver, copper and iron. Chakravartin can also be used as an epithet for Buddha whose teaching is universal and whose truth is applicable to the entire cosmos. Buddhist philosophers use this title for the universal monarch with the idea of a king of righteousness and maintainer of moral law.

Cultivation
The practices one does in order to purify karma, to purify oneself of greed, anger, and ignorance, to create merit, to generate bodhicitta and, ultimately, to achieve enlightenment.

-D-

Desire, Form, Formless Realm
See *Three Realms*.

Dharma
Typically, "dharma" is used to describe the body of teachings expounded by the Buddha. However, the word is also used in Buddhist phenomenology as the term for phenomenon, a basic unit of existence and/or experience.

Dharma King
A dharma master with a complete knowledge of the Buddhadharma.

Dharma Protector (Vajra Protector; Wrathful Protector)
An enlightened being that takes on a wrathful form and whose function is to protect Buddhist practitioners.

Dharma Realm
A state of existence, there are ten states of existence: hell denizens, hungry ghosts, animals, asuras, humans, devas, sravakas, pratyekabuddhas, bodhisattvas, and buddhas.

Diamond Sutra
An important teaching of Shakyamuni Buddha which shows that all things are ultimately empty and devoid of any inherent reality, including the idea of oneself, other sentient beings, and dharma.

Dragon King
One of the supermundane beings such as a god, asura, gandharvas, and, etc. A dragon king controls the realm of nagas and possesses great wealth

-E-

Enlightenment
Enlightenment is the translation of the Sanskrit word, Bodhi, which literally means awakened. Enlightenment is awakened to absolute reality as it is.

-F-

Five Skandhas
Skandha is Sanskrit for heaps or aggregates. The five skandhas are form, feeling, perception, mental formation, and consciousness. These are psychophysical components of a human being which when interacting together creates the illusion of self and inherent existence of self.

Five Buddhas
Also known as Five Dhyani Buddhas, the Five Wisdom Buddhas are celestial buddhas visualized in Vajrayana meditations. The five Buddhas are Aksobhya, Amitabha, Amoghasiddhi, Ratnasambhava and Vairocana. Each embodies a different aspect of enlightened consciousness to aid in spiritual transformation: (1) Vairocana Buddha - Wisdom of Ultimate Reality; (2) Akshobhya Buddha - Wisdom of Great Mirror-like; (3) Ratnasambhava Buddha - Wisdom of Equality in Nature; (4) Amitabha Buddha - Wisdom of Discerning Awareness; (5) Amoghasiddhi Buddha - Wisdom of All-accomplishing.

Four Englightened Beings
These are buddhas, bodhisattva, pratyekabuddhas and sravakas.

-G-

Ganges

Famous river in India which is a pilgrimage site for Hindus because it is believed that bathing in it washes away one's sins, cleanses you of all evil and, if one's ashes are placed in it upon cremation, the river will take you to heaven. It is frequently mentioned in Buddhist sutras since the Buddha spent a lot of time near the Ganges and many Indian people at that time could relate to the metaphors in which he used the Ganges, i.e., "the number sentient beings that would be liberated by the Buddha would be as numerous as the stars that fill the sky, like the sands of the Ganges."

Garuda

Great golden-winged birds. They are considered to be half animal and half god. They used to eat dragons from the ocean until the Dragon King pleaded to the Buddha to have him help convince the garudas to stop eating the dragons. The Buddha agreed to have all reverends make daily offerings to the garudas in exchange for not eating anymore dragons. They serve as protectors and helpers to dharma practitioners.

Geomancy (Feng Shui)

Use of astronomy and geography in placement of buildings, gardens, water features, furniture, objects, etc. to help one improve life by receiving positive energy. It is an art and science which originated in China approximately three thousand years ago.

Golden Rooster Standing on One Leg

If someone were to ask what Buddha-nature is, Grandmaster Lu said that he would join his palms together in salute and stand on one leg which he called "Golden rooster standing on one leg." This "Golden Rooster pose" is always there and not distinguishing self and other. The standing on one leg reveals a supreme truth. The palms-joined salute also reveals supreme truth.

-H-

Heart Mantra
When a buddha or bodhisattva reaches enlightenment, his enlightenment is mirrored through the frequency of his heart mantra. When one chants the heart mantra, a resonance is created which allows one to merge with that respective buddha or bodhisattva.

Heart Sutra
One of the shortest (260 characters in Chinese) and most famous sutras of the Mahayana Buddhist Sutras. It is based off the *Prajnaparamita Sutra*, which was condensed into the *Diamond Sutra*. Despite its length, it encompasses the Buddhism systemic teachings of existence, emptiness, and realization and can be described as the most profound of all sutras.

Hungry Ghosts
This is a transcription of "Preta," one becomes a hungry ghost due to greed. The body of a hungry ghost is shaped like a vase, the stomach is very wide and the neck is as thin as a pin, some of them have fire in their stomach and the fire burns whatever food they try to eat.

-I-

Illusory Body
See *Six Yogas of Naropa*.

-J-

Jade Pond Golden Mother (Golden Mother of the Jade Pond)
Ruler of all female immortals, she is the most important female deity of the Taoist Pantheon. Known by many names such as Queen Mother of the West, she came into being from the gathering of primordial yin (feminine) energy. Her palace is located on top a peak in the Kunlun Mountain Range. She represents the metal element in the Taoists Five Elements (metal, wood, water, fire, and earth) and there is a Jade Pond near her palace, hence she is also known as the Golden Mother of Jade Pond.

Jade Rabbit of the Moon Palace
A traditional Chinese legend tells us of three sages who transformed themselves into pitiful old men and begged for something to eat from three animals in order to test their characters. The chosen animals were a fox, a monkey and a rabbit. The fox and the monkey both had food to give to the old men, but the rabbit, empty-handed, offered his own flesh instead and jumped into a blazing fire. The sages were so touched by the rabbit's sacrifice that they let him live in the Moon Palace where he became the "Jade Rabbit." In Chinese mythology, the Jade Rabbit lives on the Moon where he makes an elixir of immortality.

-K-

Kalachakra (Sanskrit, literally "Wheel of Time")
This is one of the four Highest Tantra Yoga practices. It is considered to be one of the most complex pra

Karma (Sanskrit, literally "Action" or "Deed")
A foundational concept Buddhist, Hindu, Jain and Sikh traditions, it is believed that all actions, thoughts and speech generate a result. If one is virtuous in body, speech and mind, then one will have good

fortune, harmonious relationships, success, happiness, etc. If one performs non-virtuous deeds of body, speech or mind, one will suffer the consequences. The results of one's deeds, good or bay, will bear fruit in the present life or in future lives. The experiences one currently witnesses are a result of previous actions if past lives, or even from actions committed previously in this current life. Karma, or cause and effect, is what drives the cycle of reincarnation for all sentient beings.

Karmic Cause (Cause and Effect)
A foundational concept Buddhist, Hindu, Jain and Sikh traditions, it is believed that all actions, thoughts and speech generate a result. If one is virtuous in body, speech and mind, then one will have good fortune, harmonious relationships, success, happiness, etc. If one performs non-virtuous deeds of body, speech or mind, one will suffer the consequences. The results of one's deeds, good or bay, will bear fruit in the present life or in future lives. The experiences one currently witnesses are a result of previous actions if past lives, or even from actions committed previously in this current life. Karma, or cause and effect, is what drives the cycle of reincarnation for all sentient beings.

Kasaya Robes
Robes of Buddhist monks and nuns, named after a brown or saffron dye. In Sanskrit and Pali, these robes are also given the more general term "cīvara," which references the robes without regard to the color. During the early period of Chinese Buddhism, the most common color for Sangha robes was red. Later, the color of the robes came to serve as a way to distinguish monastics, just as they did in India. However, the colours of a Chinese Buddhist monastic's robes often corresponded to their geographical region rather than to any specific schools. In the Tang Dynasty, the Chinese Buddhist monastics typically wore grey-black robes, and were even colloquially referred to as Ziyi, "those of the black robes." By the Song Dynasty Chinese monks

typically wore red robes.

King Yama (Lord Yama, Yama King, Yama, Deva, Hell King)
Yama was considered to have been the first mortal who died and espied the way to the celestial abodes, and in virtue of precedence he became the ruler of the departed. Therefore, he is known as the greatest king (Lord) of the netherworld and the head of karmic arbiter giving punishment of those who reside in hell.

Ksitigarbha Bodhisattva (Sanskrit, literally "Womb of the Earth")
One of the eight mahasattvas (great beings), the bodhisattva of great vows and like all bodhisattvas, he aspires to deliver sentient beings wandering astray in the six realms (hell denizens, hungry ghosts, animals, asuras, humans, and devas), but he specializes in delivering beings from hell. He is usually represented as a standing venerated figure, holding in his right hand a pilgrim's staff, and in his left a pearl. His famous vow is "Not until the hells are emptied will I become a Buddha; not until all beings are saved will I certify to Bodhi."

-L-

Lord Indra
In Hindu mythology, he is the supreme deity amongst all the deities in the heavens. He governs the thirty-three heavens within the Trayastrimsa Heaven, which is a heavenly realm above the realm of the Four Heavenly Kings, on top of Mount Meru.

-M-

Madhyamaka (Sanskrit, literally "Middle Path")
Nagarjuna founded the Middle Way School based on the teachings of emptiness that all things are empty of inherent existence.

Mahamayuri Vidyarajni (the Peacock Dharma Protector)
An emanation of Vairocana Buddha who has the power to create harmony, increase wealth, purify negative karma and protect practitioners from disasters.

Mahasthamaprapta (Sanskrit, literally "Arrival of the Great Strength") The bodhisattva of the great power of wisdom and is often depicted in a trinity with Amitabha Buddha and Avalokitesvara Bodhisattva in the Pure Land School. They are also known as "Three Holy Sages of the Western Land of Ultimate Bliss."

Maitreya Buddha
He is regarded as a future Buddha of this world in Buddhist eschatology. In some Buddhist literature, such as the *Amitabha Sutra* and the *Lotus Sutra*, he is referred to as Ajita Bodhisattva. The name Maitreya (Metteyya in Pāli) is derived from the Sanskrit word maitrī (Pāli: mettā) meaning "loving-kindness", which is in turn derived from the noun mitra (Pāli: mitta) in the sense of "friend."

Maitreya is a Buddha who in the Buddhist tradition is to appear on Earth, attain complete enlightenment and teach the Pure Dharma. According to scriptures, Maitreya will be a successor to Shakyamuni Buddha. It is found in the canonical literature of all major Buddhist schools (Theravāda, Mahāyāna, Vajrayāna) and is accepted by most Buddhists as a statement or prophecy, about an event that will take place when the Dharma will have been mostly forgotten on Earth.

Maitreya's Cloth Sack
This refers to the bag that Maitreya Buddha is typically depicted as carrying. This image is one of the main forms in which Maitreya is depicted in East Asia. He is almost always shown smiling or laughing, hence his nickname in Chinese is the "Laughing Buddha."

Mandala (Sanskrit, literally "Circle")
It is a symbol which represents the realms of buddhas, bodhisattvas, or dharma protectors. It also represents various energies of particular enlightened states of mind. It may be in two dimensions, as in a painting, or in three dimensions, such as in the placement of sacred objects. The body or even the world at large may be interpreted as a mandala, as they symbolize various aspects of universal energies. The representations are very artistic with intricate colors and designs to aid in visualization. It also refers to a visualization of an offering multiplying infinitely into the space of the entire universe.

Manjushri Bodhisattva (Sanskrit, literally "He Who is Noble and Gentle")
He is the Bodhisattva of Transcendent Wisdom. He is typically depicted with the *Prajnaparamita Sutra* and a sword which cuts through the clouds of ignorance. His practices may be used to help gain wisdom, knowledge and eloquence.

Mantra
Chants used for blessing, invocation of buddhas, offering, harmonization, purification, protection, longevity, etc. It is a sound of sacred syllable, word, or group of words and is the embodying of spiritual power. The chanting of mantra is used as a method of meditation to create spiritual transformation. A mantra also represents the pure speech of enlightened beings, buddhas and bodhisattvas. It is one of the three secrets of tathagata (pure body, speech, and mind). In Vajrayana Buddhism, the chanting of the mantra (pure speech) is accompanied by visualization (pure mind) and mudra (pure body) as prescribed in sadhana to transform ordinary body, speech, and mind of a person to the pure body, speech, and mind of a buddha.

Middle Way (Madhyamaka)
Nagarjuna founded the Middle Way School based on the teachings of emptiness that all things are empty of inherent existence.

Mount Meru (Mount Semeru)
The proper name is "Meru" ("Neru" in Pali). "Su" is a prefix meaning "excellent" or "wonderful." It is a giant mythological mountain located in the center of the universe, it is often used as a simile for size and stability in Buddhist texts. It is shaped like an hourglass, with a top and base of eighty-thousand yojanas squared. The middle narrows to twenty-thousand yojanas squared and has a height of forty-thousand yojanas (the exact measure of one yojana is thought to be twenty-four-thousand feet, or approximately four and a half, but other accounts put it at about seven to nine miles).

Mudra (Sanskrit, literally "Seal")
It is an expression of hands and fingers that corresponds to the enlightened body of the three secrets of tathagata (enlightened body, speech, and mind). In meditational practices, forming mudra assists the practitioner to correspond his body with enlightened body of the personal deity. In application, mudra acts as a seal reinforcing the power of mantra and visualization.

-N-

Nirvana (Sanskrit, literally "Cessation")
Cessation of suffering where one is freed from the cycle of rebirth. It is a state where one realizes one's connection with the absolute.

-O-

-P-

Padmakumara (Sanskrit, literally "Lotus Youth")
The sambhogakaya (bliss body) form of Living Buddha Lian-sheng, a great fortune-bestowing and hindrance removing Bodhisattva. For more details about Padmakumara and his abode, the Maha Twin Lotus Ponds in the Western Paradise, see the *True Buddha Sutra*.

Padmasambhava (Sanskrit, literally "Lotus Born")
He is the founder of the Nyingma tradition of Tibetan Buddhism and is commonly known as the Second Buddha, after Shakyamuni Buddha. He was supremely accomplished in the esoteric arts and used his powers to defeat many demons and black magic (Bon) practitioners after being invited by the Tibetan king Trisong Detsen to establish Buddhism in Tibet in the eighth century. Padmasambhava is one of the principal deities of True Buddha School.

Pratyekabuddha (Solitary Realizer)
A practitioner who attains nirvana without a human teacher, but does not go on to teach others the path towards enlightenment.

Pure Land
A pure abode founded by a buddha. By being reborn in a pure land, the aspirant can continue spiritual development towards enlightenment without fear of falling back into the six realms of reincarnation.

Pure Land Buddhism
One of the schools of Mahayana Buddhism in which the objective is to be reborn in Amitabha's Western Paradise.

-Q-

Qi
Energy which can leak from the mind via craving, greed, anger, igno-

rance, and wrong views. To cultivate the mind is to cultivate qi, and to cultivate qi is to cultivate the mind.

-R-

Raksasi
Evil and violent demons referred to as "man-eaters." In this realm these demonic ghosts eat human flesh. Raksasa is the male version and Raksasi is the female version.

Reincarnation
In Buddhism, as in Hinduism and various other religions, it is believed that after one dies the spirit enters the bardo realm as it prepares for its next rebirth. One may be reborn in any of the six realms of samsara: hell, heaven, human, animal, asura or hungry ghost. It is also possible for an individual to reincarnate out of samsara and into a pure land, which provides an ideal environment for cultivation and meditation with the intent of reaching enlightenment. An accomplished or realized practitioner (by maintaining conscious awareness during the death process) can choose to return to samsara to continue benefiting sentient beings.

-S-

Saha World (Sanskrit, literally "Endure")
The Buddha called our world system the saha world because sentient beings in this world patiently endure immeasurable hardships while pursuing fleeting illusory happiness. The beginningless delusion obscures their minds from recognizing their sufferings and how to achieve liberation.

Sakra (Indra)
The ruler of the Trayastrimsa Heaven according to Buddhist cosmology. His full title (Sanskrit): *Śakro devānām indrah*; (Pāli): *Sakko devānam indo*, "Śakra, Lord of the Devas". In Buddhist texts, Sakra is the proper name and not an epithet of this deity; Indra in Sanskrit and Inda in Pali are sometimes used as an epithet for Sakra as "lord".

Sakra's heaven Trayastrimsa is located on the top of Mount Sumeru (Mt. Meru), imagined to be the polar centre of the physical world, around which the Sun and Moon revolve. Trayastrimsa is the highest of the heavens in direct contact with Earth. Like the other deities of this heaven, Śakra has a long, but mortal life. Inhabitants of the Trayastrimsa are really tall and live for one thousand years, of which each day is equivalent to one hundred years on earth. When one Sakra dies, another deity becomes the new Śakra.

Sakra is married to Sujā, daughter of the Vemacitrin (Sanskrit) chief of the Asuras, (Pāli) Vepacitti. Despite this relationship, a state of war generally exists between the thirty-three gods and the Asuras, which Sakra manages to resolve with minimal violence and no loss of life. Sakra is mentioned in many Buddhist sutras and is often shown consulting the Buddha on questions of morality. Together with Brahma, he is considered a protector of Buddhism.

Samadhi (Sanskrit, literally "Make Firm")
It is a non-dualistic state of consciousness where the meditator becomes one with the object of meditation, and there is no separation between the meditator and the object of meditation.

Samsara (Sanskrit, literally "Journey")
Referring to cyclic existence and the associated sufferings in Buddhist terminology. In Mahayana writings, samara refers to the phenomenal

universe and is considered to be the same as nirvana. Although this unity of samsara and nirvana seems contradictory, Mahayana traditions like the Yogacara School teaches that everything is the play of the mind. Hence, samsara and nirvana are just mental labels without any real substances. Therefore, if you ignore the physical aspects of these mental labels and only consider their true nature, samsara and nirvana are one and the same. Comprised of the six realms: (1) devas (gods); (2) asuras (jealous gods); (3) humans; (4) animals; (5) hungry ghosts; (6) and beings in hell. Sentient beings are stuck in the six realms until they attain enlightenment and realize that the realms are merely states of consciousness, thus freeing them of the need to be reborn in one of these realms.

Sariputra
Originally known as Upatisya, he was the son of a Brahman scholar. Before taking refuge in the Buddha, he had already acquired many students of his own, and he eventually led three hundred and fifty students to take refuge in the Buddha. He was renowned for his great wisdom, was the principal disciple of Shakyamuni Buddha, and the person most trusted by the Buddha. He followed the Buddha for more than forty years, during which not one single thought of displeasure or dissatisfaction with the Buddha arose in him. He entered into the tranquil realm of nirvana before the Buddha did.

Shakyamuni Buddha
Siddhartha Gautama was born in Lumbini, India (modern day Nepal) sometime between 563 BCE to 483 BCE. He later became known as Shakyamuni Buddha. "Shakya" was his clan name and "muni" means great sage, thus, "the great sage of the Shakya clan." At the age of twenty-nine he left his home, and achieved enlightenment under the Bodhi Tree at age thirty-five. He became the founder of Buddhism and spread the dharma to all beings.

Six Unenlightened Beings
These are the beings of the six realms: hell denizens, hungry ghosts, animals, humans, asuras, and devas,

Six Yogas of Naropa
These are a collection of the completion stage practices of several tantras: (1) Inner Fire Yoga (Tummo); (2) Illusory Body (Gyulu); (3) Dream Yoga (Milam); (4) Clear Light (Osel); (5) Conscience Transference (Phowa); (6) Bardo.

Sravaka (Sound-hearer)
One who attains enlightenment by being a disciple of, and hearing the teachings of a living buddha.

Sutra
Meaning "a thread that keeps things together" in Sanskrit which is the metaphor for a set of rules and principles. In Buddhism, sutras are discourses given by the Shakyamuni Buddha. Its usage has broadened to designate discourses by other buddhas such as the *Mahavairocana Sutra* or other highly regarded sacred Buddhist texts, such as the *Platform Sutra*.

-T-

Talisman
Metaphysical amulets infused with the power of the creator. They are drawn onto paper and then burned and eaten or carried by the person wishing to use the talisman's power. They may be used to help cure illnesses, offer protection from danger, create harmony in life, etc.

Tantra
Refers to the teachings of Vajrayana. It is the spiritual truth which

seeks through various mystical means to unite the individual consciousness with the universal consciousness.

Taoism (Daosim)
A philosophical, ethical, and religious tradition of Chinese origin that emphasizes living in harmony with the Tao (Dao). The term Tao means "way," "path" or "principle" and can also be found in Chinese philosophies and religions other than Taoism. In Taoism, however, Tao denotes something that is both the source and the driving force behind everything that exists. It is ultimately ineffable: "The Tao that can be told is not the eternal Tao." Thus, the Tao is the "mother" source that gives birth to and nourishes all things, the primordinal source of all beings and all things eventually return to the Tao. This is the universal law. Enlightenment in Taoist sense is the realization of this universal law of all things returning to the Tao. The Tao acts spontaneously and is natural it's effects and actions are without intention yet all things can be achieved.

"Tao Jia" is the the philosophical aspect of Taoism based on the teachings of Lao Zi's *Tao Te Ching* and Chuang Zi Taoist propriety and ethics may vary depending on the particular school, but in general tends to emphasize actions without intention, "naturalness", simplicity, spontaneity, and the Three Treasures: compassion, moderation, and humility.

"Tao Jiao" refers to the religious aspect of Taoism which embraces all Taoist Schools and movements whose aim consists of attaining immortality and longevity. Institutionalized forms, evolved over time in the shape of a number of different schools. Taoist schools traditionally feature reverence for Lao Zi, immortals or ancestors, along with a variety of divination and exorcism rituals, and practices for achieving ecstasy, longevity or immortality.

Taoism has had profound influence on Chinese culture and clerics of institutionalised Taoism usually take care to note distinction between their ritual tradition and the customs and practices found in Chinese Folk Religion, as these distinctions sometimes appear blurred. Chinese alchemy, Chinese astrology, Chan (Zen) Buddhism, martial arts, Traditional Chinese medicine, feng shui, and many styles of qigong have been intertwined with Taoism throughout history.

Tathagata (Sanskrit, literally "Thus Come One)
A synonym for Buddha. It refers to the primordially pure Buddha-nature which can neither be created anew nor ever destroyed. This nature can remain obscured indefinitely if not purified and developed.

Three Realms
The Desire Realm, Form Realm, and Formless Realm. It is another way in which Buddhism distinguishes between different modes of existence. The Desire Realm encompasses the hell realm, animal realm, human realm, asura realm, and heavens up to the Parmanirmitavasavartin Heavens. The common characteristic is that the beings in this realm are dominated by desire. The Form Realm encompasses the four dhyani heavens. The beings in this realm have renounced desire but they still have not renounced form. So, the beings in these heavens still have form and reside in celestial palaces. The Formless Realm encompasses the four formless heavens. The beings in this realm have renounced both desire and form to exist in states of formlessness.

Tripitaka
Referred to as the "Three Baskets" since these early writings were made on long, narrow leaves, which were sewn together on one side and then stored in baskets, these writings contain the teachings of Shakyamuni Buddha. The texts are divided into three sections: the

Sutras (the Buddha's sermons), Vinaya (precepts/discipline), and Abhidharma (higher level teachings). It is debated if the texts were recorded during the First Council immediately after the Buddha's Parinirvana, or in later centuries. Theraveda Buddhism uses the Tripitaka as the sole canonical text, whereas Vajrayana Buddhism also relies heavily on the tantras for teachings (e.g. Hevajra Tantra, Kalchakra Tantra, etc.).

True Buddha Quarter
The True Buddha Quarter serves as the headquarters for the True Buddha Foundation, the core governing body of True Buddha School.

-U-

-V-

Vairocana (All Illuminating Sun Tathagata; Mahavairocana)
Commonly translated as the Great Sun Tathagata, Mahavairocana means the great radiant one who illuminates all directions, symbolizing his wisdom piercing all ignorance. Vairocana Buddha is the chief of the Five Wisdom Buddhas and the Lord of the Tathagata Family. He is the embodiment of the wisdom of ultimate reality. He is associated with center direction and the element of space. The symbol of his family is the eight-spoke wheel, the symbol of the noble eightfold path.

Vajra (Sanskrit, literally "Diamond Scepter"; Dorje)
A common ritual object in Vajrayana Buddhist practices which represents a thunderbolt, or diamond, which in turn represent being indestructible. It can symbolize the male aspect of enlightenment (skillful means), whereas the vajra bell represents the feminine aspect of enlightenment (wisdom).

Vajrasattva (Sanskrit, literally "Vajra Being")
One of the most important meditation buddhas, he is depicted as having a white body holding a vajra in his right hand and a vajra bell in his left. He is the composite of the Five Dhyani Buddhas. As the great lineage holder of Vajrayana, Vajrasattva taught the Great Perfection to Garab Dorje, the first human lineage holder of the Great Perfection. Vajrasattva also initiated Nagarjuna Bodhisattva into the path of Vajrayana and taught Nagarjuna the teachings of Vajrayana. Vajrapani Bodhisattva, the Bodhisattva foremost in power, is an incarnation of Vajrasattva. Vajrasattva is also known to have the greatest purification power and the Vajrasattva Yoga can remove the worst defilements. The Hundred Syllable Mantra of Vajrasattva is very well known mantra recited by Vajrayana practitioners for purification.

Vajrayana Buddhism (Sanskrit, literally "Diamond Vehicle")
Also known as the Vehicle of Indestructible Reality and Secret Mantrayana ("Mantra Vehicle"), is a form of Mahayana Buddhism in which the guru teaches an accelerated path to enlightenment through the practices of the three secrets of speech (chanting mantras), body (forming mudras), and mind (visualization). There is a vital element of the teacher-student relationship. The respect of the teacher is extremely vital in Vajrayana because the teacher is the living embodiment of the Three Jewels of the Buddha, Dharma, and Sangha.

Among its many names, this system is called the secret mantra because the profound three secrets of the buddha (enlightened body, speech, and mind) are taught as the innate nature of all phenomena. However, this profound truth is concealed by the beginningless delusion which has obscured the minds of sentient beings and must be revealed skillfully. It is taught in secret and not shown to practitioners with mundane aspirations. It is called mantra because the three secrets are presented as it actually is which is beyond the perceptions of ordinary mind.

The Vajrayana trainings consist of two phases. In the first phase is the "generation stage." These teachings emphasize on the three secrets of the tathagatas, removing trainee's obscuration to recognize that one's own body, speech, and mind are the same as that of the enlightened body, speech, and mind of a buddha. In the second phase, the "perfection stage," the trainee learns to direct the subtle vital energy and essence within the body's energy channels to manifest great bliss, inner radiance, and emptiness. Through this experiential sequence, the obscurations of trainee are removed to recognize the innate awareness that has always been there. Through the diligent practice of Vajrayana teachings, one may dissolve the beginningless delusion and attain buddhahood within a single lifetime.

Vinaya (Vinaya Pitaka)
One of the three parts of the Tripitaka which emphasizes on precepts, discipline, vows, conduct and ethics. It creates the foundation of all dharma practices and it applies to both monastics and laity.

-W-

-X-

-Y-

Yaksa
A demon similar to a raksasa and is usually evil and violent. Some are benevolent, like in the case of the twelve yaksas who serve and protect the Medicine Buddha. They aid and protect those who cultivate the Medicine Buddha Yoga. These twelve yaksas represent the twelve vows of the Medicine Buddha.

Yin and Yang
An ancient Chinese philosophy which explains how our universe is. It is the basis of Chinese medicine, martial arts, divination techniques, and Taoism. Yin refers feminine, cold, and dark while yang is masculine, hot, and light. They are polar opposites, neither good nor bad, which come together to create balance.

Yoga (Sanskrit, literally "Union")
In Buddhism, it is a method uniting an individual self with the Buddha. It includes physical and mental exercises which help one reach enlightenment.

Yogic Response (Spiritual Response)
By practicing mudras, mantras and visualizations the respective deity invoked and the practitioner is at an equal level with the Three Secrets (body, speech, and mind) of the Tathagata, and thus possesses limitless meritorious functions. Once the practitioner merges with the principal deity, he or she gains access into the dharma realm through this single gateway.

-Z-

Zen (Chan) Buddhism
Mahayana Buddhist School that originated in China (called "Chan" in Chinese) that later took root in Japan. It emphasizes the practice of sitting in meditative absorption and de-emphasizes rituals and intellectual studies.

Also From US Daden Culture

Sheng-yen Lu Book Collection 51:
Highest Yoga Tantra and Mahamudra
Sale Price: $12.00 USD
ISBN-13: 978-0-9841561-6-0
ISBN-10: 0-9841561-6-X

Sheng-yen Lu Book Collection 148:
The Power of Mantra
Sale Price: $12.00 USD
ISBN-13: 978-0-9841561-1-5
ISBN-10: 0-9841561-1-9

Sheng-yen Lu Book Collection 154:
The Aura of Wisdom
Sale Price: $12.00 USD
ISBN-13: 978-0-9841561-4-6
ISBN-10: 0-9841561-4-3

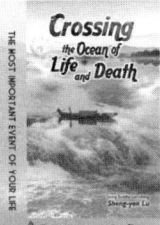

Sheng-yen Lu Book Collection 163:
Crossing the Ocean of Life and Death
Sale Price: $12.00 USD
ISBN-13: 978-0-9841561-0-0
ISBN-10: 0-9841561-0-0

3440 Foothill Blvd. • Oakland, CA 94601 • U.S.A. • www.usdaden.co

Also From US Daden Culture

Sheng-yen Lu Book Collection 166:
Travel to Worlds Beyond
Sale Price: $12.00 USD
ISBN-13: 978-0-9841561-2-2
ISBN-10: 0-9841561-2-7

Sheng-yen Lu Book Collection 200:
Pages and Pages of Enlightenment
Sale Price: $12.00 USD
ISBN-13: 978-0-9841561-5-3
ISBN-10: 0-9841561-5-1
Ebook ISBN-13: 978-0-9858080-4-4

Sheng-yen Lu Book Collection 202:
Sightings from Thousands of Miles Away
Sale Price: $12.00 USD
ISBN-13: 978-0-9841561-3-9
ISBN-10: 0-9841561-3-5

Sheng-yen Lu Book Collection 223:
Stories of Supreme Spiritual Responses
Sale Price: $12.00 USD
ISBN-13: 978-0-9858080-5-1
ISBN-10: 0985808055

3440 Foothill Blvd. • Oakland, CA 94601 • U.S.A. • www.usdaden.com

Also From US Daden Culture

Sheng-yen Lu Book Collection 129:
Entering the Most Hidden Yin-Yang Realm
Sale Price: $12.00 USD
ISBN-13: 978-0-9960699-1-5
ISBN-10: 0996069917